Virtual Reference Training

The Complete Guide to Providing Anytime, Anywhere Answers

BUFF HIRKO

MARY BUCHER ROSS

American Library Association
Chicago 2004

Composition and design by ALA Editions in Berkeley and Sans Extended, using QuarkXPress 5.0 on a PC platform

Printed on 50-pound white offset, a pH-neutral stock, and bound in 10-point coated cover stock by McNaughton & Gunn

The paper used in this publication meets the minimum requirements of American National Standard for Information Sciences—Permanence of Paper for Printed Library Materials, ANSI Z39.48-1992. ∞

Library of Congress Cataloging-in-Publication Data

Hirko, Buff.
Virtual reference training : the complete guide to providing anytime, anywhere answers / Buff Hirko and Mary Bucher Ross.
p. cm.
Includes bibliographical references and index.
ISBN 0-8389-0876-4
1. Electronic reference services (Libraries)—Study and teaching—Washington (State)—Case studies. 2. Electronic reference services (Libraries)—Study and teaching. 3. Reference librarians—Training of. 4. Reference librarians—In-service training. I. Ross, Mary Bucher, 1948– II. Title.
Z711.45.H57 2004
025.5′24—dc22 2003027440

Printed in the United States of America

08 07 06 05 04 5 4 3 2 1

CONTENTS

PREFACE

A few words of clarification may be necessary for the reader. The controversy about what to call the people who visit us—in person, on the telephone, via the Internet—still rages. Are they patrons? Users? Customers? Something else altogether? At this point in time, agreement on a moniker appears unlikely, so we had to choose one for the purposes of this book. While I personally like the term "user," since it rules out the idea of money-backing (patronage) and money-spending (customer), it has other negative connotations and seems impersonal in a way that library folks dislike. For this book and its context, we chose "customer." The reason is simple: most of the virtual reference applications in use by libraries today are based on commercial call center applications. The underlying concept behind them was to make it easy for customers to contact service or product providers; report concerns, questions, and problems; and receive a response from the organization. For better or worse, we use "customer" as the single term to describe those individuals—obviously intelligent and aware—who visit us in our myriad guises.

We also consistently refer to those who participated in our virtual reference training classes as "learners" or "participants" rather than as "trainees." The focus of our program was on learning rather than on dictating the correct or ideal way to provide virtual reference service. Libraries, communities, and staff members are so diverse that trying to tell someone how to serve a particular customer in a specific library in Wherever will obviously fail. There are too many variables involved. We don't have a better word than "training" to describe the activities of the Anytime, Anywhere Answers program outlined in this book, but our experience made it obvious that those activities have much more to do with collegial process and individual experience than with instruction. We refer to the wonderful people who joined in our program as "learners" or "participants," although even those terms fall short of describing them.

Finally, I would be remiss if I did not recognize the extent to which the Washington state library community contributed to our success. There were and are champions everywhere, from the relatively well-funded and well-staffed libraries in Puget Sound to the small and enthusiastic (but poor) systems in sparsely populated corners of eastern Washington. We have learned from them all.

BUFF HIRKO

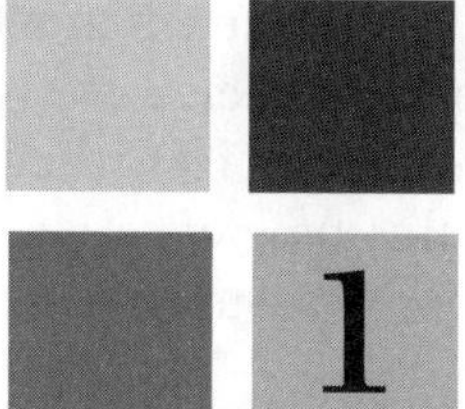

Beyond Shazam! Training for Virtual Reference

A librarian (we'll call her "Marion") participating in an exercise for an Anytime, Anywhere Answers class reported the following experience during a visit to a metropolitan public library's chat reference service. Marion's assignment was to act in the role of a parent seeking information on the safety of a 1997 Malibu she was considering purchasing for her teenage daughter. She also was to ask about laws restricting teenage driving. As her commentary reveals, her online experience was less than gratifying:

> "If I were a patron using chat for the first time, this would have been my first and only time," Marion noted. "After being connected with a librarian and asking my initial question, I waited about five minutes. Then a Google.com screen appeared. I waited a minute or two more and then sent a message that I had received the Google screen. The librarian's . . . next message told me not to type anything until she got back to me. It really put me off—felt like I was being yelled at."
>
> After keeping Marion waiting for about five minutes, the librarian finally pushed a screen for Edmunds.com. "I asked if this page would have info about crash tests and she said she didn't know and suggested I do a search on my own using Google," Marion reported. "So, I asked if Google was like Yahoo. I also asked about state laws for teenagers." The reference librarian's response? Another admonishment for Marion to quit typing until she had answered the questions. Finally, after ten minutes, the librarian tried to push another page. "It never worked and finally she sent me the URL for a site about car ratings," Marion reported. "I sat there feeling like I would have bailed if I was a real patron, but afraid to type anything in case I would get 'yelled' at. After waiting a long time again, she sent me the URL for the motor vehicle department."

What went wrong in this transaction? Many things, from the repeated instruction about not typing to the long, unexplained time lapses. Unfortunately, this exchange clearly illustrates what can—and too often does—happen when library staff members are given little or no training for reference in the online environment. In this case, Marion, the learner, acting in the role of customer, experienced firsthand the frustration and resentment that customers may feel when they use a virtual reference service. As more libraries offer this type of service without preparing their staff sufficiently, an increasing number of customers are likely to become disillusioned with it.

In their eagerness to embrace the concept of serving customers at the point of need and use cutting-edge technology, many libraries have purchased applications and have scheduled staff members to man the virtual reference desk without offering them more than a cursory introduction to the new software. At the 2001 Virtual Reference Desk Conference, Charles McClure described this phenomenon with the phrase "Shazam! You're a virtual librarian!"

But to properly implement a virtual reference program in a library, he asserted, there needs to be excellent training. As both presenters and attendees at the conference agreed at the time, a thoughtful and thorough program to prepare staff for the new, faceless, fast-paced world of web-based reference service had yet to be developed.

Enter the Anytime, Anywhere Answers curriculum.

In the spring of 2001, the Statewide Virtual Reference Project (VRS) was established in Washington to support the implementation of electronic reference services across the state. As a Library Services and Technology Act (LSTA) initiative of the Washington State Library (WSL), the project explored a wide range of issues and activities. One key component of the project was the development of a curriculum—dubbed "Anytime, Anywhere Answers"—designed to train library staff members in the effective delivery of virtual reference service.

The curriculum developers took into consideration all of the factors relevant to any library training program. Such programs must be developed in the context of people, place, time, and resources. Each of these factors affects the others. "People" include actual and potential customers, as well as those who use the training to deliver the service. "Place" can be a community, a building, a desk, or a website. "Time" can apply to training activities, service hours, individual transactions, and evaluation. "Resources" range from equipment and telecommunications to licensed databases, book collections, and money. A careful consideration of all these factors and their interrelationships is needed prior to starting a program.

The nature of the service must be examined in addition to the environmental context for training. Designing a successful training curriculum for virtual reference service begins with the recognition of the elements it has in common with traditional reference service and those that depart from the familiar. Reference service is a tool used by libraries to answer customers' information needs—a service routinely provided for more than a century. On the other hand, virtual reference service is still new enough that no common term or phrase is used to describe it: digital reference, live chat, virtual reference, synchronous reference, and more.

This book outlines not only the curriculum used by Washington State's Statewide Virtual Reference Project, but also provides the results of our learners' experiences. It illustrates both the potential and the pitfalls implicit in virtual reference. During the first year of training, more than sixty staff members from fourteen academic, public, and special libraries across the state participated in eight classes. They discovered that the lessons learned in the Anytime, Anywhere Answers program are equally valuable in other reference contexts. Good practices in clarifying the question, writing an understandable policy, providing information literacy instruction, and other procedures covered by the training also apply at the desk, on the telephone, or in the stacks.

They also found that some of their assumptions were challenged. During the first year of training classes, we discovered that library staff members held many preconceived ideas about interactive chat service: that customers expect instantaneous answers, that a typed question is a well-considered one, that Google is the tool of first choice, that an onslaught of questions will ensue if the service is widely marketed, and more. We often heard the suggestion that a staff member with good technology skills who was uncomfortable working with customers at the desk might be well suited to online reference. While some of these and other assumptions may hold kernels of truth, our training program proved that many of them are erroneous or overblown.

This volume covers the full range of issues, activities, and materials related to the development and implementation of the Anytime, Anywhere Answers training program. It provides background on the processes and components that went into the decision making that resulted in the curriculum described in chapter 7. It also offers information that can be used by administrators, training developers and instructors, reference managers, and reference staff members in libraries that are currently offering or considering virtual reference service. Among many possibilities, the guide can be used to:

- identify essentials that must be considered prior to developing or delivering a training program, such as budget, software, facilities, staff, and more
- determine the appropriate level of training for a particular library
- develop training materials and activities that meet local staff and customer needs
- select staff members to act as instructors or participate in training
- assess the effects of training on library staff members
- evaluate the quality of virtual reference service
- understand the wide range of issues and concerns inherent in virtual reference service

We begin, in chapter 2, with a brief overview of the Statewide Virtual Reference Project, because the needs of Washington libraries dictated the format and content of the training curriculum. Core competencies (chapter 3) were the foundation for the training. As indicated by the experience described in the opening paragraph of this chapter, the online environment, with its lack of visual cues and its perception of immediacy, provides a real test of traditional reference techniques. It is critical that individuals and organizations recognize the skills, abilities, and aptitudes that are fundamental to successful service. We identify a wide range of needed abilities and provide assessment tools to determine competency levels both prior to and following training.

One of the answers to the challenges we faced in Washington—geography, multitype libraries, disparate staff education and experience levels—is the use of the constructivist approach (chapter 4), which focuses on learning from the user's viewpoint and then applying that understanding in the workplace. Participants find varied ways to link new information to traditional tasks, basing their work on personal experience with digital reference services offered by other libraries. This active learner participation offers a uniquely reasoned perspective.

Chapter 5, on blending face-to-face with distance learning, reflects the need to combine the structure of the classroom with the flexibility of online resources. Utilizing multiple delivery formats reinforces learning. The value of shared observations among participants from varied library settings, when added to the desire for self-paced activities, provided an optimal learning environment.

An outline of the steps needed to initiate a training program of this type is offered in chapter 6, with emphasis on a practical appraisal of local needs and constraints, including considerations for timeline, staff requirements, software, communications, and related areas. A complete description of the learning activities and assignments included in the Anytime, Anywhere Answers curriculum is offered in chapter 7, including chat practice, multitasking skills, Secret Patron tasks, transcript review, electronic discussion list posting, Virtual Field Trips, and critiques of other online information services. We add excerpts from our learners' activity reports to illustrate their online discoveries. These also provide real-world examples of the widely varying quality of virtual reference service.

The most difficult aspect of digital reference service involves incorporating model reference interview techniques into an online transaction. In chapter 8, we offer ways to incorporate guidelines (such as those offered by the Reference and User Services Association) for setting the tone, getting the question straight, keeping the customer informed, providing information, and follow-up.

Because many aspects of digital reference service are constantly evolving, it is important to assess training from both trainers' and learners' perspectives and modify subsequent offerings in response. In addition, the evaluation process must be revisited after the training has been in use for a period of time. The last chapter suggests a variety of tools and methods for assessment, including trainer debriefings, evaluation forms, and third-party monitoring.

Following the text, a number of appendixes provide examples of course materials and learner assignments. These include course readings, self-assessment tools, a selected chat meeting transcript, Virtual Field Trip reports, Secret Patron scenarios and observations, and trainer tips. The book concludes with a glossary and a bibliography of course readings. To download some of the forms, handouts, and tools we used in the program, visit http://vrstrain.spl.org.

We will begin with a snapshot of libraries in Washington State in 2002, the place and time for which the Anytime, Anywhere Answers program was built. The challenges we faced became the criteria for training development and delivery.

Introduction: Washington's Statewide Virtual Reference Project

CHALLENGES IN WASHINGTON STATE

The state of Washington is demographically, geographically, and economically diverse. Occupying a rough rectangle at the northwest corner of the lower forty-eight states, it has a land area of 66,544 square miles—larger than all of New England—and a population of just over 6,000,000. More than half of that number live in the greater Puget Sound area surrounding Seattle. The Cascade Mountains divide the state psychologically as well as physically. Western Washington has a famously wet, mild climate and big trees; eastern Washington is dry, with hot summers, harsh winters, and big skies. Apart from the aerospace, manufacturing, and high tech firms located in Puget Sound, the state's economy largely depends upon the products of the land: agriculture and timber. Seemingly every part of this financial foundation has been hit hard over the past decade. As we know, library use rises as the economy dips.

The state's diversity is reflected in its libraries. There are 67 academic libraries in Washington and more than 230 special libraries, including 23 that serve Native American tribes. Of the state's 65 public libraries, 24 serve populations under 5,000. Almost 2,400 libraries serve public and private K–12 schools. Numbers alone fail to describe the range of communities and the services provided to them. The state's 35 two-year institutions include both community and technical colleges. Four-year academic institutions range from the very large state-supported University of Washington and Washington State University, both of which have branch campuses, to small private liberal arts schools like Whitman College and those with specialized curricula, such as the Art Institute of Seattle. Public libraries serve metropolitan cities like Seattle and Spokane, sparsely populated rural counties like Pend Oreille, small towns such as Concrete, and every sort of community in between. Staff experience and education levels vary widely, and a number of small libraries operate without a postgraduate-degreed librarian.[1]

STATEWIDE VIRTUAL REFERENCE

Against this backdrop, the Statewide Virtual Reference Project (VRS) was established in the spring of 2001 as a Library Services and Technology Act initiative of the Washington State Library. The VRS Steering Committee established the project goal: "Combining the power of libraries, librarians, and technology to help all Washingtonians get information wherever they are." This was a tall order in a state where collaboration among libraries traditionally has been resisted. (There is no state funding for public libraries. Geographic diversity and distance, wide variation in size, uneven distribution of wealth, and divergent service areas [municipal, county, regional] create jurisdictional obstacles that are difficult to overcome.) The top priorities for VRS were assessing needs that related to digital reference service across the state and opening a grant cycle for demonstration projects, closely followed by a carefully conceived training program. These would establish and reinforce the collaboration needed to fulfill project goals.[2]

In order to provide a snapshot of electronic reference service in the state, a postcard survey was mailed to every library in fall 2001. Sixty-one percent of public, academic, and special libraries and 30 percent of K–12 libraries replied. The results were heartening. More than half of the responding public, academic, and special libraries provided both websites and e-mail reference service to their customers. But at that time, only one Washington library—King County Library System—offered live, online digital reference service. The state was well poised to expand, enhance, and connect electronic information services, from e-mail to live chat and evolving technologies.[3]

Even more interesting were the results of four focus groups of potential virtual reference customers held across the state. These gatherings were one of the initial needs-assessment activities for the VRS Project. Our purpose was to get the candid views of citizens on their preferred ways to interact with libraries in order to answer their information needs. The results were posted to the Web to assist libraries receiving grant funds in the development of responsive services.[4] Reentry workers in Port Angeles (located on the Olympic Peninsula with its troubled timber industry), Hispanics in Monroe (an agricultural center northeast of Puget Sound), and senior citizens from Bellevue (Seattle's affluent neighbor to the east) gathered in person, and a large group of teens assembled in an online chat meeting. There was a remarkable consensus among these very different groups on several points. Few realized the range of services and materials—either general or electronic—available at their local libraries, all urged libraries to advertise and market, and all recognized the "fast food mentality" that emphasizes a quick response to customer needs. Further, many echoed a baker in Port Angeles who noted that his information needs often came at 3:00 A.M. We are a 24-hour, 7-day-a-week society whether we like it or not.

FALL 2001: COLLABORATIVE ENERGY

Training development was initiated by the Best Practices and Training Subcommittee of the VRS Project, representing a mix of library interests: Nancy Huling, University of Washington; Joan Neslund, Ellensburg Public Library; Barbara Pitney, King County Library System; Mary Ross, Seattle Public Library;

and Buff Hirko, Washington State Library. This group's first conclusion was that training needs took precedence over best practices. The January 2002 opening of the grant cycle would necessitate training to support successful demonstration projects. These projects would generate best practices.

We began by identifying those aspects of training that are the foundation for any good Internet-based reference service. These included skills necessary to search the Web and databases, use software, and understand patron cues in an online environment. These skills were viewed as a subset of training that also includes general reference and information literacy. We recognized both a universal need for training and for tailoring it to specific staff and locations in order to accommodate local experience, equipment configurations, and available resources.

In a moment of common inspiration, we realized that an ideal tool for delivering electronic reference training to remote library staff members would be an interactive chat/web-browsing software package. Not only could librarians train in familiar surroundings, but it would be a cost-effective technique. For staff members with little or no experience with text-based chat, it would provide practice in this new online environment.

We quickly moved to listing areas that were critical to high-quality digital reference service. We assumed that vendors would provide software-specific training, and therefore we would not address that need. This proved to be a wise decision for several reasons. By the time training actually began in fall 2002, four different vendor products were being used in Washington libraries, with others under consideration. Furthermore, the need to develop consistent skills for all institutions offering digital reference services proved important in increasing trust among staff members at partnering libraries, and in providing common quality standards in collaborative settings. Subcommittee members identified the following skills, aptitudes, and knowledge as critical in the online environment:

1. Chat skills
2. Online reference interview
3. Internet searching
4. Database searching
5. Collaborative browsing
6. Customizing scripts
7. Methods for evaluating success
8. Coping with technical glitches

The group recommended that participants complete a self-assessment test in order to evaluate their abilities and determine whether additional training would be necessary prior to working directly with customers.

RESULTS

The VRS Steering Committee endorsed the subcommittee's recommendations enthusiastically, and in April 2002, the Statewide Virtual Reference Project contracted with the Seattle Public Library (SPL) to develop a training curriculum for delivery to Washington libraries. The anticipated start date was September 2002. The development team included SPL's Mary Ross and Daria Cal, and Emily Keller, a graduate student at the University of Washington's Information School. This remarkable trio produced the Anytime, Anywhere Answers curriculum, closely following the guidelines outlined by the subcommittee the previous fall.

The Statewide Virtual Reference initiative focuses on the development of best practices, methods, and standards for creating virtual reference services, with the ultimate goal of establishing a statewide collaborative electronic reference system. Guidelines for grant demonstration projects encourage partnerships to explore a wide range of activities, from testing software and developing online tools to implementing homework help and multilingual service. In 2002, seven LSTA grants were awarded by the WSL to an interesting variety of partnerships. The University of Washington and the King County Library System, which use two different software vendors to provide live digital reference service, developed marketing program guidelines. Tacoma and Highline Community Colleges explored the most effective methods for using digital reference service to meet the needs of students enrolled in distance learning courses. The Seattle Public Library, King County Law Library, and the University of Washington Health Sciences Library formed a consortium to provide distributed reference service. Washington State University-Vancouver and Clark College tested live chat as a means of delivering information literacy instruction to distance learners. Skagit Valley College (in Mount Vernon, north of Puget Sound) and Grays Harbor College (on the southwestern coast) used live digital reference as part of their role as inaugural sites for the statewide community college Virtual Campus.

Spokane and Spokane Falls community colleges, along with public library systems in three rural counties—Stevens, Whitman, and Pend Oreille—tested the collaborative use of live chat. The three county libraries also received a grant to market the service to their communities. This five-library cooperative effort is especially interesting for virtual reference service. It not only mixes academic and public institutions, but also provides service over the northeast corner of the state, where weather and distance separate libraries from the customers they serve. The community colleges serve distance students as well as metropolitan Spokane. The public libraries in the group have many small branches in which paraprofessionals provide reference services.

The second electronic reference survey completed in late 2002 identified twenty-eight libraries offering live, online digital reference service as well as an increasing library web presence. Moreover, the need for the training program has continued to grow.

For our curriculum designers, the challenges were multiple. The training had to address concerns such as:

- software neutrality for applications provided by different vendors
- content appropriate for staff members from libraries serving communities of differing size and characteristics
- a shared learning environment
- a wide range of education and experience levels
- focused pre- and post-training assessment tools
- program delivery for remote learners

Budget and time constrained these requirements. VRS is an LSTA-funded project with finite funding, expected to end in federal fiscal year 2004. Focusing on skills related to the delivery of quality reference service rather than software-dependent expertise helped us to avoid some of the pitfalls of trying to keep up with ever-changing applications. Still, we needed to provide timely readings and current web resources for both trainers and learners. The curriculum would require constant review and updating in order to prepare learners for real-world developments.

Many perspectives nourished the program, both directly and indirectly. The value of mixing staff members from multitype libraries was demonstrated in other training workshops conducted by the WSL. The VRS Steering Committee represents a broad range of library interests, giving voice to the needs of small, rural, K–12, and special libraries as well as those of large public and academic institutions. The Train the Trainer workshop held in September 2002 produced both great enthusiasm and keen observations from a group of talented librarians. Many staff members at both the Seattle Public Library and the Washington State Library contributed ideas and support.

By June 2003, eight classes had completed VRS training. Adjustments were made, based on the experiences of both trainers and learners in the first sessions, and more are expected as the program proceeds. And so the collaboration continues, from the beginning around a conference table to chat sessions across the state; from committee members, development team, and trainers and learners to customers. Like other aspects of virtual reference service, VRS training is a work in progress—but it is one with the potential for both profound evolution and improvement. Beyond the service itself, it will strengthen library cooperation and provide incentives to collaboration. In an era of dwindling resources, these are significant benefits.

Anytime, Anywhere Answers was implemented to support virtual reference services in the broad context outlined above. Curriculum development began with a closer examination and definition of the core competencies identified by the Best Practices and Training Subcommittee. This is the subject of the next chapter, which is the entry point for the exploration of virtual reference service training.

NOTES

1. *2001 Directory of Washington Libraries* (Olympia: Washington State Library, 2002).
2. 2001–2002 VRS Steering Committee members: Eileen Andersen, Washington Library Media Association; Buff Hirko, Washington State Library; Jean Holcomb, King County Law Library; Nancy Huling, University of Washington; Joseph Janes, University of Washington; Linda Malone, LaConner Regional Library; Verla Peterson, City University; Barbara Pitney, King County Library System; Matthew Saxton, University of Washington; Liz Stroup, Timberland Regional Library; Lou Vyhnanek, Washington State University; Jan Walsh, Washington State Library; Jonalyn Woolf-Ivory, Sno-Isle Regional Library.
3. For complete results of the survey, see the "Electronic Reference Inventory," Washington State Library, Statewide Virtual Reference Project, at http://wlo.statelib.wa.gov/services/vrs/currentactivities.cfm.
4. For the complete report on the focus groups, which offers insights into a broad range of library operations as perceived by customers, see Patricia L. Owens, "Focus Group Results: March 2002," Washington State Library, Statewide Virtual Reference Project, at http://www.statelib.wa.gov/libraries/projects/virtualRef/activities/.

3 Core Competencies: Knowledge, Skills, and Aptitudes Needed for Virtual Reference

The online environment, with its lack of visual cues and its perception of immediacy, provides a real test of traditional reference techniques. It is critical that individuals and organizations grasp the skills, understanding, and aptitudes that are fundamental to successful service. The Anytime, Anywhere Answers curriculum recognized a wide range of needed abilities and provides assessment tools to determine competency levels both prior to and following training. In this chapter, we will discuss each of these competencies.

The competencies identified by the Best Practices and Training Subcommittee in fall 2001 provided the basis for those incorporated into the training curriculum. Along with a review of virtual reference literature and consultation with colleagues, the developers attended library conference programs and participated in relevant training opportunities. These experiences expanded the list, and the following competencies were used in the final training package:

1. Ability to derive professional satisfaction from virtual reference transactions
2. Keyboarding proficiency
3. Communication skills and etiquette for chat, e-mail, and other online interactions
4. Ability to conduct an effective reference transaction in online environments, including the creation and use of pre-scripted messages
5. Internet searching skills, in particular the ability to choose the best starting points for online searches
6. Ability to effectively search and demonstrate searching of library databases
7. Knowledge of licensing restrictions connected with the use of library databases
8. Ability to assist online users in applying critical thinking skills in locating, using, and evaluating information
9. Ability to effectively conduct a collaborative browsing session with a patron

10. Evaluation of online reference transactions and identification of improvement strategies
11. Multitasking and managing multiple windows; effective use of Windows keyboard commands and shortcuts
12. Technical troubleshooting skills and ability to explain technical problems to facilitate diagnosis and solution
13. Ability to create and apply reference transaction policies in an online environment (e.g., scope of service, time limits, obscene callers, harassment)
14. Commitment to continuous learning and motivation to improve skills in all areas of reference services

Early in the process, the training developers realized that the curriculum could not address directly all of these identified needs. If an individual lacked certain skills, such as keyboarding, he or she would not be able to participate in training until proficiency was attained. Some, like multitasking and online chat skills, require practice in order to achieve expertise, and the training was limited to introductory activities. Knowledge of technical troubleshooting and software features is variable, since it relates to applications and equipment in use at the local library. While the training raised the awareness of the need for competency in these areas, they were beyond the scope of the curriculum. Tips and techniques were offered to aid efficient use of Windows. Online tutorials were recommended for learners who wished to improve their Internet reference search skills. The primary focus of Anytime, Anywhere Answers was on facilitating ways to answer customers' online information needs in the most effective way.

PROFESSIONAL SATISFACTION IN VIRTUAL REFERENCE

Like keyboarding skills, it is hoped that this core ability is present in learners prior to participation in training. This is a subjective measure of competency and may be identified by an individual or by supervisors when considering whether to participate in training. Those learners who will be most successful in providing virtual reference service already like Internet searching, enjoy the challenge of new technologies, and are willing to explore alternative reference techniques. There has been much discussion about whether good face-to-face interpersonal skills are critical online and whether those who are uneasy or impatient with public service might be more comfortable in the anonymity of online work. The experiences of learners who participated in the Anytime, Anywhere Answers curriculum's Secret Patron activities (see chapters 7 and 8) indicate that a lack of interpersonal skills—welcoming, friendly, interested communication—is easily identified online and contributes to unsatisfactory reference transactions. Certainly those who dislike using computers are unlikely to become enthusiastic about online reference service.

KEYBOARDING PROFICIENCY

Text-based chat requires ease with QWERTY keyboards. If a potential virtual reference service provider lacks typing skills, he or she must acquire them prior to beginning either training or delivery of service. Software and classroom courses are widely available to improve this basic skill.

ONLINE COMMUNICATION SKILLS

Online chat rooms and instant messaging are popular communication tools. Teenagers in particular are avid chat users. Library staff members may be comfortable with e-mail communication, but for many, text-based chat is a completely new experience. It is difficult to abandon a lifetime habit of scrupulous attention to grammar, punctuation, capitalization, and spelling, but effective chat technique operates on altered rules. It takes time to construct a grammatically correct sentence and correct spelling or punctuation. While the virtual librarian edits a response, the customer is staring at the screen, wondering whether he has been abandoned.

Effective chat technique involves several components, some of which can only be acquired with practice. Economy of phrase is invaluable, along with the ability to break a longer answer into brief one- or two-line parts that can be quickly sent. Avoiding the use of library jargon is even more important online than at the reference desk, since there is little evidence of the customer's age or familiarity with libraries. An understanding of netiquette is crucial as well, not only to ensure that the reference provider will use appropriate online behavior, but also to provide a yardstick by which to measure unsuitable customer conduct. A thoughtful policy can address many of these concerns and can also offer a guide for citation, referral, and other common online needs.

In addition to chat technique, it is important to understand related online communication modes such as e-mail. When a chat session is insufficient or inappropriate to the length or complexity of the customer's request, it may be followed by an e-mail message or phone call. The ability to provide complete, accurate, and concise information is relevant to all reference work.

Although the VRS training was not designed to provide extensive chat practice, orientation day activities included an hour of introduction to and use of instant messaging (IM). Learners were paired and given sample questions that they used as the basis for a one-on-one practice session. Those who had no previous experience with IM were encouraged to use it at home. The curriculum also provided a document titled "Norms for Online Meetings" that described pointers for successful chat.

EFFECTIVE REFERENCE PERFORMANCE

Many facets of reference service online go beyond communication skills. Open questioning, paraphrasing, and clarification of questions help ensure an understanding of the information need and create customer confidence. Good listening skills—the ability to sense underlying concerns, emotional overtones, and other unstated or unclear factors—are as important online as in person, although they admittedly are more difficult to practice. Education and experience are ongoing processes that provide the knowledge of information resources in a variety of formats and efficiency in locating them.

Pre-scripted messages, or scripts, are among the most commonly used methods of speeding and directing chat discussions. The library staff member selects appropriate responses to common questions and situations from a drop-down list of words or phrases. Scripts range from initial greetings and prompts for added information to search instructions and technical messages. Chat software may provide both institutional and individual scripts. Learners in the VRS training program commented on both the quantity and quality of scripts during chat transactions. Lengthy, formal scripts were seen as impersonal, and overuse of them implied lack of either interest or interview skills on the part of the library operator. Adding the customer's name or other quick personalization of a script ("Hello, Bob. How can I help you?") reduces the robotic feel of canned phrases. It is not uncommon for customers to ask whether they are chatting with a "real person." The ability to effectively interweave newly typed messages with scripts improves with experience.

In many respects, the Anytime, Anywhere Answers curriculum incorporated techniques used in the Effective Reference Training program offered through the Washington State Library since 2000. The difference in the VRS training was that participants were not given a formula for using the model reference behaviors, which include:

setting the tone—offering a personal greeting, providing clear interest and willingness to help, integrating scripts thoughtfully

getting the question straight—clarifying questions, using open probes

keeping the patron informed—offering instruction in finding answers, jargon- and opinion-free responses, progress reports, description of procedures, technical help

providing information—identifying authoritative, appropriate information; providing sufficient time to explore the request; citing resources; asking whether more is needed; recognizing when follow-up or referral is necessary

follow-up—asking whether the information provided is satisfactory or there are other questions, expressing appreciation and encouraging further use of the service, and requesting an evaluation of the experience

In addition, learners were required to read the Reference and User Services Association (RUSA) guidelines and apply them to the Secret Patron activity, in which they evaluated virtual reference service from several libraries. (See bibliography.) In this exercise, as well as in the evaluation of actual transcripts, they were asked to decide whether they received good service based on specific criteria, including those listed above. In all of this, participants were encouraged to construct a methodology that would work best in their personal library situation.

Those interested in this competency should read chapter 8 for a detailed discussion of methods used to incorporate model reference behaviors into the VRS training program.

INTERNET SEARCH SKILLS

Skillful searching on the Web is an integral aspect of virtual reference service. Early virtual reference services provided at-home operators with a basic library of print resources, such as an almanac and dictionary, but found that they were unused. In general, libraries report that a very high percentage of chat queries are answered with Internet resources. It follows that efficient searching is a high priority. In addition, the operator should be able to describe search steps and techniques or instruct the customer in their use. This is especially important in academic (both K–12 and undergraduate) settings, where the emphasis is on instruction in the use of resources rather than the provision of a direct answer.

Internet searching covers a broad range of skills, including:

- familiarity with browser features and functions
- familiarity with the strengths and shortcomings of various search engines and ways in which they return results
- knowledge of advanced search techniques, including Boolean operators, proximity searching, locating specialized formats such as images and sounds, and accessing the "invisible Web"
- ability to evaluate websites for authority, currency, navigability, completeness, bias, and relevance

VRS training did not attempt to provide instruction in effective Internet searching because of the range and complexity of skills required. However, two online tutorials were recommended for those wishing to improve their skills. Continuing education courses in Internet searching are widely available, both in the classroom and online.[1]

DATABASE SEARCH SKILLS

While some common skills are involved in searching the Internet and using local databases, there are also significant differences between these two types of resources. Periodical databases vary widely in structure, content, and features. Academic and special libraries use a broad range of topical databases that require specialized knowledge and offer detailed data. Sharing these resources with customers means that virtual reference service providers must understand licensing restrictions related to proprietary databases, since violating such agreements has significant repercussions.

Online library catalogs are also diverse. Virtual reference software packages are increasingly incorporating the ability to view and search the library catalog with the customer. This requires that the library staff member be proficient in using catalog features and functions and also be able to provide instruction to customers, since they routinely may access the catalog remotely on their own.

These skills obviously are beyond the scope of VRS training, since they depend upon locally available reference tools. However, nearly all of the vendors who provide databases offer training, either on-site or online. This training should be offered on a regular basis to staff members, given both personnel turnover and changing software applications and database content. State libraries, regional consortia, and other library associations often provide scheduled training for these services.

INFORMATION LITERACY

Virtual reference is a wonderful delivery mechanism for information literacy instruction. The sheer volume of information on the Web, coupled with its lack of organization and control, provides a wealth of resources both useful and awful. Providing guidance in navigating, finding, using, and assessing those resources is one of the most meaningful and satisfying responsibilities of an information professional. Virtual reference software applications that offer co-browsing or application-sharing capability are especially well-suited to information literacy instruction, but even basic chat sessions can provide learning opportunities. Asking the questions "What have you found?" or "Where have you looked?" offers an opportunity to engage the customer in thinking critically about resources that she located on her own. Comparing and contrasting sites that provide information about the same or similar topics can also illustrate their validity and pitfalls.

Anytime, Anywhere Answers provided an online chat meeting for each class that focused on information literacy, using a slide presentation to direct discussion. In addition, several readings explored the topic, as well as a link to the Association of College and Research Libraries' "Introduction to Information Literacy" web page (see the bibliography). Learners also completed Virtual Field Trip exercises in which they assessed the branding, accessibility, scope of service, authority, and confidentiality policies of a variety of virtual reference service sites. The criteria used in evaluating those web pages exemplified many of those that are key to information literacy.

COLLABORATIVE BROWSING

Not all virtual reference software provides co-browsing capability, but those who do utilize an application that offers this feature need to understand its uses and potential. Co-browsing allows the customer and reference provider to view each other's online entries and actions as they navigate and search the Internet, databases, online forms, and other resources. This is a valuable means of instructing customers in the efficient and effective use of time spent online. However, co-browsing requires practice to use it effectively and understand the effect on the customer's screen of keystrokes and commands entered by the operator.

The VRS training chat meetings used the 24/7 Reference software, which offers co-browsing; participants were exposed to it briefly. Some learners also experienced the feature during Secret Patron transactions. Relevant preparation in using this feature falls in the realm of software-specific training.

TRANSACTION EVALUATION AND IMPROVEMENT

One of the most powerful tools provided by virtual reference is the transcript of operator-customer chat transactions. Reading the actual words and URLs exchanged offers unprecedented opportunities for evaluating and improving reference service, both at an individual and institutional level. While transcripts do not illustrate the passage of time when either the customer or operator is waiting for the other to respond, they do provide an explicit record of the quality of service. Both admirable and poor reference interviews offer lessons. The participants in VRS training used available transcripts of their own Secret Patron exercises and also were given a number of transcripts from actual public and academic library chat transactions. (Identifying information about both individuals and institutions was removed from the latter.) Using a checklist of evaluation criteria, they critiqued the documents for the behaviors outlined in "Effective Reference Performance" earlier in this chapter (see appendix B).

MULTITASKING ABILITY

Efficient multitasking is the product of experience, experimentation, and personal knack. It is aided by a solid understanding of Windows features, keyboard commands and shortcuts, and mouse techniques. The complexity of actual use depends upon the sophistication of the virtual reference software being used, the volume of chat queries handled by a single provider, and the location at which the service is practiced. While virtual reference operators ideally should work away from the public service desk, it is not always possible—especially in small libraries. Handling in-person and virtual reference questions, or a combination of telephone and virtual queries, can be stressful. Some library staff members can balance two or three online customers at once without difficulty, but for most, it is challenging at the least and may be highly stressful.

At the initial orientation session, Anytime, Anywhere Answers provided an eight-page guide titled "Keys to Organizing Your Virtual Reference Desk" (see appendix G). This covered a range of tips and techniques related to desktop real estate, keyboard shortcuts and commands, mouse use, browser features, and search engine tricks. Many learners reported that they kept a copy of this beside their computers at work for ready reference and noted improvement in their keyboarding speed and Windows navigation.

Every version of Windows includes a Help file that is accessed from the Start menu. This is an excellent source of information, as are the many online tutorials available. Windows user manuals have been produced by a number of publishers for every version of the software; check your library catalog!

TECHNICAL TROUBLESHOOTING

There is no substitute for experience in this area, as is illustrated by repeated exposure to the "blue screen of death." Virtual reference service provides ample opportunities for all manner of problems, from equipment failure and telecommunication limitations to software bugs and frame-busting websites. Many libraries have developed scripts that deal with common troubles like proxy server authentication and known error messages. Unfortunately, these are matters that must be resolved locally. In terms of competency, technical troubleshooting skills are gained through experience and training in the library. This is not to underestimate the value of such abilities, however. Telephone numbers, e-mail addresses, and URLs that provide connections to technical assistance should be readily available in an online list, in a paper resource next to the workstation, or preferably both.

CREATING AND APPLYING POLICIES

The online environment can be a challenging one, and it is critical that libraries establish policies that define the scope of service, confidentiality, use of licensed databases, eligibility for service, time or transaction limits, unacceptable behavior, and related issues. While virtual reference operators often must use personal judgment in unexpected or unusual situations, they will be most successful if guided by official policies and procedures. Many of the policies applicable to virtual reference are extensions of existing ones, but there are also new concerns. How will licensed databases be shared with patrons of other libraries in a collaborative network, or those outside the library's jurisdiction? Will time limits be imposed on individual transactions? Will anonymous transactions be supported? These issues are complex and must be determined at the local or cooperative level, as appropriate.

Nonetheless, there is no reason to start from scratch unless a library's administration or board believes that is the best approach. Many policies governing both library staff and clientele are published on the Web. VRS training participants explored the policies and procedures used by a variety of virtual reference services. They selected services to visit from a table of choices, assessed them for quality and completeness, and then posted their impressions to the class discussion list (see chapter 7). As with other such postings, the trainers summarized and commented on the most thoughtful insights. This process provided learners with both a broad overview of policy considerations and concrete examples of specific concerns. It also gave them skills that could be used at their local library in reviewing or writing rules and guidelines for service.

COMMITMENT TO CONTINUING LEARNING

The speed at which both virtual reference service and the Web are evolving requires that anyone who works in the online environment be prepared to update their knowledge and skills on a regular basis. Software upgrades add new functionality, search engines improve, hardware capabilities expand, websites proliferate, and customer visits increase. Libraries must provide adequate, if not ample, training opportunities for virtual reference staff members. Individuals should stay abreast of relevant issues through reading library literature and discussion lists such as DIG_REF, and by attendance at workshops and conferences.

Anytime, Anywhere Answers emphasized continued learning throughout the course. Both trainers and learners posted citations for newly published articles or websites to the class discussion lists. Chat meetings frequently considered hot topics and ways to learn more about them. Information about training opportunities and conference programs was shared. Many learners returned to their libraries and enthusiastically recommended that their colleagues participate in future VRS training classes. In the Washington experience, the commitment to continued learning was unanimous.

SKILLS ASSESSMENT

Several evaluation tools were used to help determine the level of skills that learners brought to the training, as well as reviewing the extent to which those skills were retained. Prior to beginning class, a checklist of "Internet Reference Competencies" was mailed to each participant. This checklist was developed at the Seattle Public Library, where it was used as a self-assessment tool for staff members. Class members completed the checklist and brought it to the orientation. It was not collected, but rather was used by the participants to evaluate whether there were areas in which they needed to improve their skills. The checklist covered many aspects of Internet use, from Boolean searching and browser knowledge to search engine and site evaluation. In the checklist, participants are given response choices to "I am able to" accomplish three dozen competencies, ranging from "No" to "Easily" (see appendix A).

Participants also completed a related self-assessment of "Windows Multitasking Competencies" during the orientation, prior to the discussion of tips and techniques for organizing the virtual reference desk described earlier in this chapter. Again, this was designed to help learners estimate their ability to accomplish specific tasks, such as using keyboard shortcuts and clearing cache. This gave them a fair evaluation of their overall competence related to Windows.

During the orientation, each participant also completed the "Initial Skills Assessment of Competencies for Virtual Reference." This list of eleven basic statements asked participants to assess their confidence in demonstrating skills related to virtual reference. The lists were collected after completion and submitted to the project coordinator. Three months after finishing the class, an electronic version of the list ("Follow-up Skills Assessment") was e-mailed to each participant. While the same eleven statements were repeated on this assessment, a section was added that asked learners about their use of training skills on the job. The results of this follow-up questionnaire offered an impressive appraisal of the usefulness of the Anytime, Anywhere Answers program. All but four respondents reported that they were using 25–75 percent of the skills they were taught in the training. Of the four exceptions, one reported using only 10–25 percent of learning, while the other three reported using 100 percent. (The latter were taken more as compliment than reality.) See appendix A for copies of all these evaluation instruments.

THE NEXT STEP

After the curriculum developers identified and defined these core competencies, they examined ways in which library staff members could enlarge and improve their own abilities and skills in the online environment. Given the diversity of libraries involved in virtual reference service across Washington and the varying levels of staff experience and education, they selected the constructivist approach as the most appropriate methodology. Chapter 4 explains constructivist learning, its benefits, and its application in VRS training.

NOTE

1. Joe Barker, of the University of California at Berkeley, provides a regularly updated tutorial in web-searching skills at http://www.lib.berkeley.edu/TeachingLib/Guides/Internet/Findinfo.html. Debbie Flanagan provides practical exercises in search strategies at http://home.sprintmail.com/~debflanagan/main.html.

4 Learning through Using: The Constructivist Approach

One of the answers to the challenges of training staff members with wide-ranging levels of education and experience from all types of libraries is the use of the constructivist approach. Constructivist learning may seem like one more education buzzword, but it simply means that learners form knowledge and meaning for themselves.

When designing the curriculum for the Anytime, Anywhere Answers program, the designers had a couple of options for their approach: they could define the desired outcomes either in terms of specific behaviors or by describing different ways in which learners should be able to think about and solve problems. These two approaches to training are often contrasted as behavioral or constructivist.

The principal difference between the two approaches to instructional design lies in focus and results. The behavioral approach concentrates on immediate, measurable changes in performance, i.e., behavior. The constructivist approach combines relevant activities with a personal, social context to produce long-term changes in perspective and problem-solving abilities. In a constructivist approach, trainers provide resources, activities, tasks, and interactions that lead to exploration, discovery, and reflection. They specify the problems to be addressed and activities to be shaped by the learners, followed by ways in which the learners can reflect on the results in a group setting. In effect, the training leads learners to construct their own knowledge and meaning, leading to a set of best practices for their individual libraries.

The developers of the VRS training curriculum determined that participants would learn more effectively by reaching their own conclusions about how best to deliver service. In order to accomplish that, Anytime, Anywhere Answers was designed to allow learners to focus on exploring and thinking about virtual reference from the user's viewpoint and then applying that understanding in the workplace. Just as their personal experiences as library users inform their in-person reference skills, their experiences of virtual reference from the user's perspective enhances their ability to perform this new service.

In the VRS training program, trainers avoid lecturing on the preferred ways to practice. Instead, they encourage learners to reflect on and create best practices by observing what other staff members in other libraries are currently doing. Certain exercises, such as the Secret Patron activity (discussed more fully later in the chapter) and website evaluations, help learners determine for themselves those behaviors that work and those that fail in the virtual reference arena. This active learner participation offers a uniquely reasoned perspective.

The VRS curriculum designers defined clear outcomes for the library staff participating in Anytime, Anywhere Answers. Naturally, the primary outcome was that the learners acquire the knowledge, skills, and aptitudes identified in the core competencies for virtual reference. This led directly to a second outcome—formulating best practices for service in their libraries. Through statewide training, communities of libraries willing to collaborate in virtual reference would emerge, as well as would staff and administrators willing to share experiences and expertise. Individual and group participation would allow learners to benefit from the insights of others and enjoy the real-time chat groups, instant messaging, and online meetings. Gaining skills, deciding on best practices, collaboration, learning together, and having fun while doing it—those were the intended outcomes of the training. Training together was also a trust-building experience for those who later collaborated in virtual reference services—a benefit that was not initially predicted. In addition, it made participants tolerant of the inevitable technical glitches and scheduling problems that occurred during classes. Trainers and learners worked together comfortably and amiably. The curriculum goals shaped the content by providing learners with a picture of how they would profit from the training. They also shaped the format and approach used.

The curriculum developers knew that the learners were motivated by a common interest in establishing or enhancing virtual reference services and that their learning would be defined by their own service context. It was important to provide an opportunity for them to define their own goals for the training. They did this by jointly deciding on due dates for assignments and dates for online meetings. In a variety of activities, the learners were given choices about how to structure the actual activity. Their postings to the online discussion lists were guided by questions that emphasized what they had discovered and how it would be applied in planning and implementing service at their own libraries. The training itself provided a structure of multiple interactions (learner with content, learner with trainer, learner with learner). Through them, they would acquire new perspectives on virtual reference.

WHAT DOES CONSTRUCTIVIST LEARNING LOOK LIKE?

Constructivist learning encourages the exploration of both real-world and simulated environments that exemplify the issues and practices in digital reference. It allows the learners to decide which key aspects of the service need to be examined, based on their personal experiences and workplaces. In the Anytime, Anywhere Answers curriculum, this was accomplished through several activities.

In the *Virtual Field Trips,* learners chose the library websites they would explore from a grid that identified libraries by type, the software used, and the services offered (e-mail and/or chat). They answered a series of questions about the branding, accessibility, and scope of the reference service. Then they summarized their impressions for the discussion list, guided by questions such as "What were your overall impressions, as a patron, of the sites you visited?" and "What did you observe that you want to remember in planning and implementing your VR service?" By reviewing a number of library websites, from user-friendly to poorly designed ones, learners then were able to view their own libraries' web presence with a critical, more balanced eye.

Secret Patron activities provided the learners with specific scenarios to use in real-time interactions with three different virtual reference services. They then compared and contrasted the responses and service received from each library. The scenarios described a type of patron, an information need, and an "escalator" question that starts with a general inquiry, then progresses to a specific one. In later classes, the trainers decided to encourage learners to compose their own Secret Patron scenarios, based on the examples provided. This led to some lively discussion about the way that library patrons ask questions. For each interaction, they evaluated the effectiveness of the reference interview, the appropriateness of the answer, and gave their overall impressions of the service received. It is worth noting that reference service professionals are frequently more critical of their colleagues than customers would be. They are more likely to comment on failures to clarify the question or identify an authoritative source. Again, the wide variety of service quality and scope provided a much-needed look at virtual reference from the user's perspective.

Weekly chat meetings provided learners with opportunities to share their reflections on readings and activities with other training participants. These meetings focused on key topics: Information Literacy in Virtual Reference, Service Evaluation and Improvement, and Marketing of Virtual Reference. Using chat-based online meeting software also gave the learners valuable experience with a communication tool similar to the instant messaging used by many of their virtual reference patrons. Experiencing the same technical problems and limitations that users encounter offered learners a valuable understanding of—and sympathy for—the customers they meet in chat reference sessions.

A key ingredient of constructivist learning is the facilitating role of the trainers. During the face-to-face orientation, they led each group in deciding due dates for assignments, as well as dates and times for online meetings. They presented a preview of the training, provided hands-on experience with chat and online meeting software, and gave some tips for success in distance learning. During the five weeks of the distance learning course, their roles were to:

- Support and encourage the learners, providing technical assistance whenever needed.
- Facilitate an active, collaborative environment through comments to the discussion list.
- Guide the online meetings.
- Provide formative feedback to the learners on their completed assignments.
- Ask the right questions rather than give the right answers.

In all of this, interactivity was critical to success. The constructivist approach recognizes that there are multiple ways to solve problems. Encouraging learners and trainers to share opinions on an equal footing means that they will recognize alternative perspectives and a range of techniques for delivering service. In the orientation, online chat meetings, and postings to discussion lists, learners and trainers exchanged questions and comments freely. This was invaluable in the Washington classes, each of which was made up of learners with highly diverse backgrounds. A typical training session included staff from public libraries, community college and university libraries, a county law library, and a private university.

The constructivist approach was new for nearly all of the trainers. During the Train the Trainer workshop, background about this approach was provided to the trainers (see chapter 7 for a complete description). The training designers emphasized the need to listen to and build on the questions and comments of class participants. Using this approach, the trainers learned along with students rather than positioning themselves as experts. A community of learners would be established at the very beginning of the training.

With a learning methodology in place, the curriculum developers turned to the problem of delivery format. As noted in chapter 2, one of the challenges to VRS training in Washington is geography. Our learners would come from libraries in all corners of a fairly large state. Addressing the complexity of the core competencies meant that training would be spread over an extended period of time. Finding a way to establish collegiality among participants and also provide independent learning opportunities resulted in a blend of delivery modes for the training, as outlined in the next chapter.

5 Multiple Ways of Learning: Face-to-Face and Online, Individual and Collaborative

One of the major obstacles to developing a statewide training program is delivery. Because Washington's Statewide Virtual Reference Project includes libraries located in the far reaches of the state, keeping learners engaged was a challenge. Distance learning educators report that the completion rate for online courses is discouraging. While the experience or skill level of a student may play into the likelihood that he or she completes a course, student dropout has no particular tie to locale. From the beginning, we recognized a need to combine the structure of the classroom with the flexibility of online resources.

The curriculum developers decided to blend several training methods on the assumption that no one method is ideal, and all provide benefits for learners. The strength of the VRS program lies in a combination of experiences—in the classroom, in chat meetings, in self-paced online activities, in offline reading, in sharing observations with classmates and trainers via electronic discussion list. Anytime, Anywhere Answers began with an all-day in-person orientation, followed by five weeks of varied activities. Learners participated in one hour of online chat meeting per week. They completed other activities at their own pace, and there was wide variation in the quantity and length of postings to the discussion lists. A complete description of the curriculum structure is provided in chapter 7.

IN-PERSON TRAINING

There are obvious advantages to face-to-face (F2F) training. Above all else is human contact: real people, real voices, real questions, real reactions. Learners can connect personally with instructors and fellow participants, and common experiences and interests are shared. Learners see others who, like they, are reluctant or lack confidence; alternatively, they encounter potential helpers and expert resources. In some cases, it's a chance for a star to shine. The opportunity to meet colleagues from other libraries of differing types serving contrasting but nearby communities is invaluable. The developers of the curriculum realized how crucial this face-to-face experience would be to the participants, devoting a full day of orientation to classroom learning (see chapter 7).

The classroom is also a familiar setting, one in which there is an expectation of exchanged knowledge and skills. With luck, learners arrive anticipating something new and different. A thoughtful approach to training can take advantage of this positive attitude. By interacting in a classroom setting, participants can discuss, and dispel, some of their apprehension about the nature of online reference—the perceived need to provide instantaneous responses, the lack of physical cues about customer concerns, the sheer volume of web resources.

Furthermore, when introducing learners to the online environment of virtual reference, it is important to offer hands-on help, be it from trainers or other participants. When learners observe others who are either embarrassed or delighted by their own skills, their own barriers to learning drop. In an early VRS class, the only person who was familiar with the Windows logo button was a middle-aged rural library director working toward her M.L.S. degree in a distance learning program. Expertise dwells in unexpected places.

Another advantage to F2F training is the free flow of questions and commentary. In an arena as new as digital reference, both of these tend to be wide-ranging. The participants in VRS training brought a broad array of skills, experiences, educational levels, and expectations to the classes. For example, one class partnered trainers from a large state university and a metropolitan public library, while the learners included staff members from a county law library, two different urban public library systems, and a private university focused on distance learning. All brought unique perspectives and contrasting needs, offering unexpected observations and welcome humor. Individuals met colleagues working in dissimilar settings, all located in the same metropolitan area. This exposure to staff members from other libraries "across town" was one of the most-valued aspects of training reported by participants in the WSL's Information Literacy Program workshops of 2001–2. In the case of learners representing libraries bound by a cooperative agreement, this is a trust-building exercise. One of the most frequent comments heard in collaborative services is "we're just not sure that Whosit Library is up to our standard of service," or some similar statement of doubt. Meeting, training, and sharing experiences with cooperative colleagues can go a long way toward easing such skepticism.

At the same time, it is important to recognize the disadvantages of F2F training, which are mostly logistical and financial. It may require time away from work, including travel. For institutions that are minimally staffed and unable to support travel expenses, this can be onerous. A commitment to high-quality virtual reference service must be accompanied by a willingness to put staff, resources, time, equipment, and energy to the best use. No activity is more likely to contribute to success than thoughtful, thorough training.

ONLINE TRAINING

That's what this is all about: *online*. There is no substitute for firsthand experience with the bumps, delights, frustrations, surprises, and agonies of the Web. If the Web's peccadilloes can frustrate the experts in libraries, how must they provoke the poor souls who log on with expectant innocence? Imagine learning that the online legal expert you trusted is fifteen years old, or that there really aren't whales that mistakenly wandered into Lake Michigan, as one website purported. Imagine what it's like to act on the assumption that the online information was accurate and then suffer the consequences.

To offer training in digital reference service that does not include an online component would be foolish, but it is important to consider what sort of online elements are both necessary and practical. The skills needed to successfully negotiate the Web will be identified in a later chapter. This discussion focuses on the kinds of online experience that offer value for training library staff members in delivering effective, efficient reference service via computer.

Given that a library's staff will be trained in the software provided by a digital reference vendor, what other online knowledge is needed by staff members in order to deliver good service? This was one of the questions the VRS training curriculum developers asked. First, virtual reference service operators would need to understand the environment used by their customers. That means experiencing chat, surfing library websites, using search engines and directories, posting messages, and otherwise exploring the Internet. A number of different techniques and resources can be used to provide this experience. Software is available for a variety of online uses, including the following:

web publishing, which allows content to be publicly posted on the Internet

course management software, which provides tools to organize syllabi, readings, assignments, surveys, tests, student data, and other elements of distance learning classes

meeting software, which offers a method for multiple individuals to communicate in real time via text-based chat, with the bonus of a transcript of the proceedings

instant messaging, which is just that—a way for two (or more) individuals to send messages to others who are online at the same time

electronic discussion lists, which automatically broadcast e-mail messages to all subscribers on a mailing list

blogs (*web logs*), which are web pages that serve as a publicly accessible journal, usually related to a specific topic and updated regularly

e-mail management, which provides the ability to collect, organize, and answer messages—including distribution, referral, status tracking, and statistical reporting

interactive chat applications, which are the focus of VRS training: they allow library staff members to communicate with customers in real time, using text-based chat and an array of features such as pushing web pages, using scripted messages, recording transcripts, and sharing Internet browsers

These applications range from free to expensive, and new features and packages appear at an alarming rate. Any of these applications has potential for online training; each must be evaluated in terms of cost, equipment needs, usability, relevance, timeliness, technical support, and documentation. See chapter 6 for a more complete discussion of these issues.

For the Anytime, Anywhere Answers program, three primary online tools were used. The complete curriculum was published to several pages (both for trainers and learners) on a website. An electronic discussion list was established for participants in each class. Weekly chat meetings were held using two different tools—first, a free instant messaging program, then the meeting feature of an interactive chat program.

By publishing the entire course content online, learners were able to access it "anytime, anywhere," as promised. In the first classes, which took place in November–December 2002, participants came from Colville (in the northeasternmost corner of the state), Everett (north of Seattle), Colfax (an hour south of Spokane), Bellevue (in the heart of Puget Sound), and beyond. One glance at a map of Washington State explains why a web-based course was a necessity. It is also worth noting that when the original Train the Trainer workshop was held, participants unanimously recommended that the Anytime, Anywhere Answers website be security protected. Trainers agreed that the quality and quantity of published content should be protected in order to maintain control over access and ensure that appropriate credit was given for any reuse of materials.

One aspect of online resources required close attention and review. Many of the activities required visits to library websites. Two different grids were developed that provided relevant information on these sites: the library name and location, website URL, type of service offered, hours of operation, and types of online policies and procedures. This information was subject to frequent change, resulting in several updates during the course of the training months. Posting and maintaining the data is labor-intensive but necessary work.

For most of the duration of the VRS training program, two classes ran concurrently, with a separate electronic discussion list established for each. This allowed learners from the group that participated in the face-to-face orientation to post and comment on assignments. Some of the discussions were exceptionally lively, as in certain critiques of Secret Patron activities or library websites (see chapters 7 and 8 for examples). The electronic discussion lists also provided a mechanism for trainers to guide discussion, make observations, and offer additional resources.

Chat meetings offer a number of benefits. In some cases, learners enter the training with little or no experience using online, text-based chat. Gathering participants in an "online room," where the only communication form is chat, forces them to use the same tools—keyboard, mouse, monitor—that are used by their customers. For many, it's a revelation. These meetings also provide real-time contact with other members of their training class. Personalities make themselves known in chat meetings through wit, incisiveness, thoughtfulness, and unexpected insights. Trainers can ask pertinent questions to develop topical discussions. For all VRS chat meetings, topics and agendas were prearranged. Each meeting focused on a single aspect of virtual reference, such as information literacy, the reference interview, evaluation and improvement, and policies and procedures.

VRS meetings that used the free instant message format were somewhat problematical. No formal topic was assigned; rather, the objective was to offer the opportunity to get comfortable with the chat environment—the speed, acronyms, confusion. This format, used in the first chat session for each class, did exacerbate frustrations for those new to it. A limit on characters in the text box was annoying for many learners. In most cases, no transcript was available. Only two or three questions and answers were displayed, making the discussion difficult to follow. Without the ability to share documents, web pages, or other topical cues, it was difficult to maintain structure. The success of these meetings was largely dependent on the makeup of the class. More experienced chat groups had better outcomes. On the other hand, most agreed it was worthwhile to experience this "real-world" environment, which is routinely encountered by customers.

To guide and organize the sessions, the trainers used the meeting feature of an interactive chat application designed for virtual reference delivery. The curriculum developers incorporated a slide presentation, accompanied by scripted questions and comments that invited reactions. Each participant automatically received a transcript of the entire meeting, including URLs for slides. Because there was no need for note-taking, trainers were able to participate fully. Each VRS class was limited to ten registrants in consideration of the difficulties inherent in conducting online meetings of large numbers of people. The two trainers were assigned separate tasks: one logged on as the meeting operator, pushing slides and pre-scripted messages to the attendees. The other logged on as a participant, controlling the discussion, encouraging brainstorming, and drawing out themes. All of these online get-togethers were interesting; some were insightful or provocative (see appendix F for an example). In the best ones, participants connected observations from class readings with online activities or personal experience in virtual reference transactions.

Most problems encountered during these sessions were related to equipment and telecommunications. This was especially true for those using older computers and dial-up connections, but also for individuals using institutional computer labs where software restrictions were in place.

INDIVIDUAL LEARNING

All learning is individual, whether one is part of a group or working alone. Understanding ways in which learning can be optimized is the trick. The important consideration in the VRS training program was balancing personal with group learning, as well as choosing which activities were best served by each method. Individual learning can be self-paced within the overall course timetable, while group activities require a mutually accepted schedule. The advantages of a solo pursuit include the ability to divide it into logical chunks that adapt to one's own style and speed, to review or repeat puzzling or interesting topics, and to augment personally intriguing experiences.

Anytime, Anywhere Answers provided several types of individual activities. Readings pertinent to each week's focus were both required and recommended. One of the toughest jobs for curriculum developers and training administrators was to ensure that the list of readings (see the bibliography) was reviewed and updated to reflect currency, accuracy, and relevance. By definition, virtual reference is evolving both as an operational service and as a technologically based one. Perspectives and priorities are constantly changing, and it is critical that the training program provide inclusive, balanced views. Both trainers and learners helped in this effort, pointing to outdated resources and suggesting new ones.

Another consideration for web-based training of short duration is that readings be readily available, preferably from either web-based sources or widely used full-text databases. The VRS training program ran for five weeks, which provided minimal opportunity to locate and use interlibrary loan materials. It also is important to select articles that can be digested in reasonable time frames and to limit the number of required readings. A number of background articles were given a "recommended" status either because they were difficult to locate or because they enlarged on issues already mentioned in the required readings. All participants in the VRS training program either were employed or were enrolled in graduate studies. As enjoyable and interesting as the training was, it created stress in weekly work schedules.

Several other activities were completed individually. By definition, Secret Patron exercises required a single learner to act out scenarios via a real-time transaction with a remote library staff member providing virtual reference service. Each participant was asked to conduct three such sessions with different libraries so that they could compare and contrast services. In Virtual Field Trips, individuals explored and evaluated library websites to determine best practices. Once again, three sites were assigned. In the last week of class, learners individually visited library websites that provided online policies and procedures, assessing their content for quality, clarity, and completeness.

All of these individual activities allowed learners to extract those aspects and issues that were most relevant to their personal aptitudes and experiences, and also to their local library's resources and community. The most significant obstacle lay in workplace scheduling. Prior to beginning class, each participant was given an outline of the curriculum that included an estimate of time required to complete the activities and assignments. It was emphasized that class tasks should be considered part of the normal workweek rather than an added duty. Registrants were encouraged to talk with their supervisors and colleagues, sharing information about the class and arranging work schedules that accommodated it. Nonetheless, many participants found it difficult to fit VRS training into their weekly library calendar.

COLLABORATIVE LEARNING

No facet of the Anytime, Anywhere Answers program was more fascinating than the interaction of learners from different library environments. Libraries of every type were represented: large, medium, and small public ones; large and small, public and private, two- and four-year academic; single-building and multiple-branch systems; metropolitan, suburban, and rural; law, military, state. The value of exposure to ideas and concerns from another institutional or community setting is inestimable. There are distinct differences in emphasis from one type of library to another. Academic libraries focus on instruction, helping students to work independently in locating appropriate resources. Public libraries try to find the best answer to the customer's question. Special libraries have several perspectives. Medical and law library staff members clarify the customer's need and help locate appropriate resources, strictly avoiding interpretation of content, while corporate libraries work to find both definitive resources and answers. The VRS training classes held in eastern Washington provided an opportunity for staff members from five libraries cooperating on a grant demonstration project to work together. They came from three county rural libraries and two community colleges and shared a license to provide virtual reference service to a sparsely populated, large area surrounding Spokane. This has been one of the most successful grant projects to date.

Learners' interaction began with the Getting Ready for Training orientation day, which started with a get-acquainted exercise, Walking Billboards. Each class decided collectively on three or four areas of personal interest (e.g., hobbies or favorite foods), and individuals listed their preferences on a poster-sized paper that was taped to their shoulders. Then they mingled, reading the posters and conversing about the choices on each list. One group considered ways to be pampered, which elicited much laughter. The focus of all activities throughout the day was interaction. Trainers encouraged questions, answers, and observations from the attendees. A hands-on preview of chat meetings provided both opportunities for paired participants to communicate with each other and for the entire group to send and receive messages. The day ended with a group discussion of the steps that would follow, incorporating both curriculum requirements and suggestions for easing training activities at the workplace. Through these interactions, participants grew familiar and comfortable with each other. For the remainder of the course, they would be working with people they knew.

The online chat meetings and electronic discussion list postings that occurred throughout the following weeks provided additional valuable collaborative opportunities that reinforced the orientation day experiences. In turn, these online sessions were more open and cooperative because the participants had established relationships with each other during orientation. Learners could match real faces and voices with online names. All of this reduced the invisible, often artificial barriers between staff members working in libraries of different sizes and types and gave meaning to questions and comments.

The only real barrier to collaborative activities is managing the attendees' diverse work schedules in order to meet online at a predetermined time. Setting a schedule for weekly meetings was one of the most important tasks completed during the orientation day. Inevitably, some learners missed some of these sessions, but for the most part, attendance was very good throughout each class.

In summary, one of the great strengths of the VRS training program was its blend of individual exercises and collaborative opportunities. Staff members who have worked in only one or two libraries, possibly similar ones, benefit greatly from working with those in a different setting. Hearing alternate techniques and exploring issues from contrasting viewpoints contributes to the ability to choose from a range of responses when the unexpected occurs in a chat session. We know that customers come from every conceivable background. One size does not fit all, and the willingness of library staff members to react with flexibility is a big plus for customer service.

These beginning chapters cover the major issues that went into development of the Anytime, Anywhere Answers curriculum. In the next chapter, we offer a list of suggestions and options that can be used to develop a local training program for virtual reference service. It is not exhaustive, but it does provide a range of considerations—resources, time, software applications, and more. Washington's VRS training program selected from these possibilities; your library, staff, and community may dictate different choices.

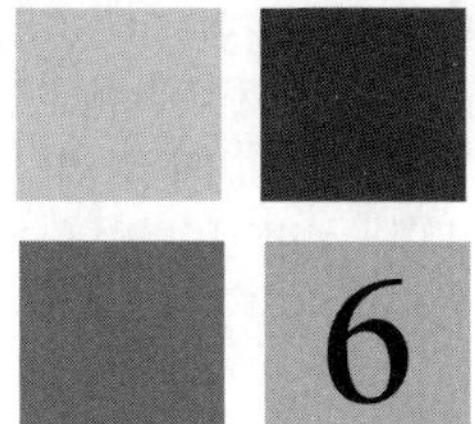

6 Getting Started: Curriculum Development

Up to this point, we have discussed the development of and the theory behind the Anytime, Anywhere Answers curriculum. In this chapter and those that follow, we will turn our discussion to some of the practical matters involved in creating and running a virtual reference training program. We will detail our experiences conducting the Anytime, Anywhere Answers program, from designing and refining the curriculum to the tools we used. We will also offer advice gleaned from our experiences and reflections on service delivery from our trainers and learners.

In this chapter, we'll look at how you can get started on training for virtual reference service in your library. The training considerations and issues discussed here should provide insight into both the necessities and possibilities for developing a program from scratch. In the following chapter we will provide a complete description of the program we delivered in Washington. If you use our model, you may also want to use or modify the many training tools provided in the appendixes as a starting point for your own exercises, forms, and questionnaires.

ASKING THE IMPORTANT QUESTIONS

Once the decision has been made to implement a live, online digital reference service, a critical priority is staff development. Devoting time, money, equipment, and people to a service as complex as online reference must be accompanied by the willingness to prepare staff for the new environment. The "Shazam!" model is uncomfortable for many reasons. Online experience and skills usually are distributed unevenly among staff members, as are interpersonal skills and knowledge of information literacy techniques. If the service is a cooperative one in which two or more libraries share resources, the need for consistent, thorough training becomes even more acute. As stated earlier, good training is a powerful tool for establishing trust in the service quality of partner institutions. It lowers barriers to collaboration.

A number of questions must be asked prior to the development of any training curriculum. What are the budgetary constraints? Who will coordinate the program, and what staff support will be needed? Who will deliver training, and how will they be prepared for the work? Which and how many staff members will be trained? What is the time frame for completion? What content is needed to ensure staff competence? How and where will training be delivered? What equipment, software, and facilities will be needed? What ongoing communication methods will be used? How will success be determined? Within each of these questions are underlying queries and assumptions. At this stage, practicality and efficiency are deciding factors.

BUDGET

As a baseline for comparison, appendix H details the costs of developing and delivering eight Anytime, Anywhere Answers classes between March 2002 and June 2003. A total of sixty-four learners and ten trainers participated.

One of the advantages of participating in an LSTA development project is that the Institute of Museum and Library Services requires that applications provide detailed information about the anticipated use of grant funds. For small libraries with limited staff, the applications are a blessing in disguise. The proposal process forces careful consideration of many things, especially money. If grant funds are involved, the budget bottom line is probably predetermined. Matching funds may be specified. No project is limited to the funds delineated by grant requirements, but few libraries are able to augment that money by any substantial amount. For collaborative services, funding probably will be shared. Determining who will pay for what is an early consideration.

In terms of training, costs vary. An existing curriculum may be purchased or licensed. If it is modified locally, additional staff time means added expense. A curriculum developed entirely in-house involves many factors: staff hours, software licenses, telecommunication costs, printing (for course materials), telephone bills, travel costs, and more. Trainers may be hired either internally or independently. Facilities may be rented or located in the funding libraries; at the least, overhead costs must be considered. All of these expenses are related to the length of the training program. The more extensive the program, the higher the costs. Similarly, the overall expenditure increases with the number of participants, although the per-person cost of curriculum development decreases.

Course content published to a library website involves room on a server, a license for design software, and staff time for development and publishing. If the curriculum is obtained from another source, server capacity is still required. More important, web pages must be monitored in order to maintain currency, either for content updates or underlying software requirements. Like housework, the job is never finished.

Training time allocated to staff who will be away from their regular duties must be considered. Will substitutes be required? Is it possible to reschedule staff to accommodate training needs? Staff time—a line item in every budget—cannot be ignored. Librarians who are designated as trainers will need additional hours to develop knowledge and skills that are transferred to others. The Anytime, Anywhere Answers program required all trainers, who were full-time employees of several Washington academic and public libraries, to participate in a one and a half-day workshop that introduced them to the curriculum, software, and course requirements. Beyond that, there were stipulations to conduct a full-day F2F orientation and weekly online meetings, review and comment on electronic discussion list postings, and evaluate learner participation in consideration of awarding completion certificates. Thirty work hours were estimated as necessary for each trainer to complete the program activities for a single five-week class. (This closely approximates the time needed for learners' activities and assignments.) Most trainers used annual leave in order to participate and were compensated from LSTA funds. A training program developed in-house could use normal library staff hours—but those aren't free, either. Time devoted to training is time taken from other tasks, for both trainers and learners.

There are two ways to determine a training budget. One is to list all possible items with their associated costs and compute the maximum total. That amount can then be compared to the funds actually available. The list can be prioritized and paired until the bottom lines of both amounts match. Alternatively, a list of costs for a minimal program can be developed, and elements can be added until the program equals available funds. Examples of ways to limit costs include:

- using web-publishing software currently owned by the library rather than purchasing a more sophisticated package
- using freeware applications for electronic discussion lists, chat meetings, blogs, and other online functions
- holding F2F sessions in a library computer lab in a central location to reduce travel
- incorporating training materials that are available at no cost from web resources
- selecting trainers from local staff with previous training experience
- limiting readings to materials available online
- requiring learners to print course materials locally
- eliminating graphics from locally designed content
- reducing the length of training classes
- training a limited number of staff who will train others on the job
- sharing training with one or more other libraries

These are just a few ideas. The single most important cost is human: good trainers will contribute more to the success of the program than any other element, along with the time spent by staff in acquiring needed skills.

PROGRAM MANAGEMENT

Training requires a great deal of coordination. A good manager must possess excellent organizational and communication skills, logistical knowledge, familiarity with available resources, knowledge of budgets, and a commitment to timeliness. There are several steps in the training process, and each requires careful planning. Training must be developed, delivered, and evaluated. The training manager must also be flexible in the face of crisis. Equipment problems, illness, traffic disasters, and similar emergencies may require changing schedules or finding substitute trainers or facilities.

Training development may include evaluating, selecting, and purchasing software and course materials; hiring, contracting with, or selecting staff to prepare a curriculum; obtaining server space; providing training for the trainers; and establishing evaluation tools and techniques. Training trainers includes many of the elements required for training delivery: selecting an instructor, scheduling time and facilities, distributing announcements, preparing workshop content, and compiling and reproducing materials. Training delivery also requires a number of decisions, such as class size, determining experience or skill prerequisites for participants, registration methods, mode of delivery (online, F2F, or a combination), establishing program target dates, and establishing criteria for certification if offered.

One incentive for training completion is to offer learners continuing education credit units. This option was explored for Anytime, Anywhere Answers but proved too difficult to implement in the time frame available. Coordinating training between two or more government agencies created unforeseen problems. VRS training was administered by the state library and offered at multiple locations across the state. Distance learning educators from higher education institutions were contacted. Bureaucratic obstacles included the fact that program administrative responsibility lay outside college or university control, as well as determining procedures for establishing fees, completion criteria, and similar official needs. Establishing continuing education credit for training as extensive as the VRS program is certainly worthwhile, but it is a lengthy process.

Training can't take place without learners. Classes must be announced in a timely manner to an appropriate audience. Because we believed that the classes would be most beneficial to those who were currently providing virtual reference service, announcements were made selectively. A series of e-mail messages was sent to representatives from grant project and other Washington libraries offering live interactive reference, beginning six weeks in advance of each class. Information included dates and times, locations, the intended audience, time requirements, and a brief description of the course, week by week. One such message read:

> The Statewide Virtual Reference Project announces the next round of "Anytime, Anywhere Answers" training for virtual reference providers: Tuesday, April 15, Seattle Public Library Annex, from 9:00 to 5:00.
>
> The training is intended for staff members of libraries either currently delivering or considering real-time digital reference service—also termed live chat. Typically, an individual library registers 2–3 librarians in a class. In most cases, the first librarians enrolled from any given library have been the most skilled and experienced staff members. The diversity of libraries represented in the classes, with their varying perspectives, has been a very positive experience. Each class is limited to 10 trainees. The training has received national attention for its unique user-oriented approach and emphasis on core competency-based skills. Learners from past classes are reporting that the

training has wide use beyond chat reference, such as evaluating customer service, websites, and library policies.

There is no charge for the training, and any Washington library may participate. Libraries are asked to share their experiences with the Statewide VR Project on request.

The training starts with a face-to-face orientation day, after which trainees are given assignments and participate in online and self-paced activities over a five-week period:

Week 1—orientation, readings, discussion list sign-up
Week 2—(information literacy focus): online chat meeting, readings, Virtual Field Trips
Week 3—(reference interview focus): online chat meeting, readings, Secret Patron activities
Week 4—(evaluation focus): online chat meeting, readings, checking out the competition
Week 5—(policies and procedures focus): online chat meeting, readings, policy questions

More information about the training program is available at http://wlo.state lib.wa.gov/services/vrs/training.cfm.

Please send the names and e-mail addresses of staff members wishing to participate in the training directly to me. If you have questions, please contact me directly. I appreciate your attention and interest.

For each VRS training class, the project coordinator sent letters to supervisors notifying them that individuals had completed the course, as well as issuing certificates of completion and publishing the names of graduates on the Statewide Virtual Reference Project website.

When the program is completed, the manager must implement the chosen evaluation methodology. This may include scheduling debriefings, mailing surveys, compiling questionnaire results, making follow-up phone calls, and writing a complete program report. Although overall responsibility for a training program should be assigned to an individual, it is important that the decision-making processes are shared. This can be accomplished by ongoing consultation with an advisory group, colleagues, and trainers. The VRS training program's success proved the benefits of brainstorming, consideration, and review by people with widely differing perspectives.

TRAINERS

There are distinct differences between training and teaching. While individuals may be adept at both, it should not be assumed that experience with the one equates to expertise with the other. Training is meant to provide and improve skills needed to become proficient in specific tasks. It is short-term, directed toward learning facts and procedures, which may change (e.g., technology). Teaching is broader, with the goal of stimulating independent thought and imparting universal concepts, which learners apply in new ways over a lifetime. Good trainers focus on answering the needs of learners in the provision of effective virtual reference service rather than expanding scholarly knowledge. Listening and verbal skills are equally important in training.

Individuals who will deliver virtual reference training need the same competencies that are needed to provide digital reference service, as well as the ability to communicate facts, tips, and techniques. Specifically, trainers need expertise in:

- using computers, especially applications based on Windows
- searching the Internet and proprietary databases
- understanding model reference behaviors
- using online chat, including acronyms and effective communication techniques
- applying critical thinking to the use of online resources
- offering online information literacy instruction
- troubleshooting technical problems online
- understanding library policies and procedures that relate to virtual reference transactions
- conducting classes, with an emphasis on interaction with learners
- evaluating learner assignments and activities
- reporting results of classroom and online activities

Not all trainers come with a full repertoire of skills. The most effective training at this level includes an opportunity to learn about the specifics of the program, as well as providing either peer review or expert critique of abilities. In the Train the Trainer workshop that preceded Anytime, Anywhere Answers, much time was devoted to sharing comments and suggestions. In addition, the workshop instructors were expert in offering techniques for and guidance in successful training methods. Listening skills were emphasized, as were ways to restate questions, enlarge topics, ensure participation by all class members, and reinforce important threads of discussion. The best trainers incorporated these techniques into their classes with ease.

How many trainers will be required? Again, this depends upon the length of each class, as well as the size and number of classes. The VRS program contracted with ten trainers from academic and public libraries across Washington. Each class employed a pair of trainers. Preference was given to partnering representatives from different library types with contrasting experience, a practice that proved highly beneficial. By offering different viewpoints, they provided learners with alternative ideas, a range of service choices, and anecdotes from contrasting settings. Pairing eased the burden of conducting the eight-hour orientation day, dividing the agenda between the trainers according to personal interest and ability. The trainer pairs also divided responsibilities for monitoring and evaluating class assignments, guiding chat meetings, and providing encouragement to individual participants.

The VRS training program gathered an enthusiastic group of repeat trainers. The combination of the curriculum, diverse learners, and the resulting observations that came from posted assignments proved irresistible. Both trainers and trainees were alternately thoughtful, provocative, creative, surprised, and glum. The collective experience was almost uniformly positive, although individual exercises often were not. For both groups, this was an exceptional learning opportunity.

STAFF

The VRS program assumed that staff members selected for training were those who were either currently providing virtual reference service or would do so in the near future. In the Shazam! model, folks end up at the keyboard accidentally. Some of them are comfortable, others decidedly are not. Libraries with limited staff may need to assign individuals to the service even when online reference is not their preferred environment. In such cases, good training is essential. Familiarity with procedures and understanding of service objectives go a long way toward reducing stress. For libraries with the luxury of choosing which staff members will become digital reference operators, it is equally beneficial to provide them with the training and tools for success.

Who is best suited to provide live, online digital reference? Arguments abound. Will the shy person with inept interpersonal skills who excels at the computer shine in this new environment? Will the librarian who is expert with the in-person reference interview be equally successful online? Can training fill the gaps for those who are technically, verbally, or socially challenged? The jury is still out. Until we have more experience with this new environment and have evaluated the ways in which it is implemented, we won't know. Meanwhile, we can only provide the most comprehensive, thoughtful training possible in order to level the playing field.

One observation may be fair. Those who volunteer for this assignment are more likely to be open to its potential for extended customer service. Those who are reluctant when asked to participate cannot be assumed to be poor candidates—they may only be insecure about computer skills or related issues. Those who are adamantly opposed to participation should be considered a low priority for training, unless staffing levels will require them to be service providers. Turning protesters into advocates is difficult work.

In any event, requirements for participation should be established for potential trainees. There are basic skills that are needed to begin: keyboarding, understanding of Windows commands, and knowledge of reference service. For VRS training, all of the work built on these essentials, meaning that staff members who lacked them were expected to improve their skills prior to starting class. Staff members recommended by supervisors and directors for participation in Anytime, Anywhere Answers were assumed to be proficient in the necessary abilities.

TIME

The length and comprehensiveness of a training program depend on the resources available to support it and the level of staff need. Anytime, Anywhere Answers was developed on a fairly robust budget and was aimed at a broad audience. It should also be noted that the developers were highly productive librarians with complementary experience in training methodology and online techniques, including software expertise. This program was created from the ground up, producing a detailed curriculum and extensive online materials over a five-month period.

The timeline established for each class was based on providing a thorough exposure to several primary aspects of virtual reference service: chat and related online skills, information literacy, the reference interview, policies and promotion, and evaluation. It also included time for both pre- and post-training assessment. The course delivered these elements over a five-week period, with some flexibility built into the schedule. In many ways, this was an optimal—and optimistic—design. The first pairs of classes (two were held concurrently) were scheduled between November and January. There was a sense of urgency—we were anxious to deliver training as soon as possible to grant project libraries, whose LSTA funding would end the following September. Not surprisingly, the holidays proved challenging.

The timetable for any training depends upon the amount of content that will be included, as well as the intended audience. While the VRS training program was meant to be comprehensive, it would be reasonable to divide training into separate workshops for different service elements (information literacy, the reference interview, etc.) delivered over an extended time period, or to condense it into a one-day whirlwind. Another variation would be a workshop that introduces virtual reference to supervisors and administrators rather than front-line operators. The VRS project developed additional workshops that introduce virtual reference to decision-makers and library staff not currently delivering the service. There are different requirements in each of these scenarios, primarily dealing with focus and level of detail. Training aimed at a particular audience—e.g., community college librarians or rural public library staff members—may be streamlined, using familiar software and known resources. If everyone involved is part of the same institution and the computer lab is in-house, travel time will be eliminated. For any virtual reference training, some sort of hands-on experience should be included. There is no substitute for seeing the real thing.

Chapter 5 explained the advantages of blended learning. By definition, this approach requires more time. Placing the entire curriculum online can reduce the time frame, although the results may not be as successful due to the lack of personal interaction. Conducting all of the training in a one-day classroom experience will provide F2F help, but shortchanges the unique opportunities offered by online exercises. There are several ways in which VRS training time could have been reduced:

- limiting or eliminating reading assignments
- limiting Secret Patron, Virtual Field Trip, and other online activities to a single instance of each
- eliminating the instant message chat meeting
- reducing the number of chat meetings
- and reducing the orientation session to a half-day of activities (eliminating such elements as Walking Billboards and the introduction to IM chat)

Although making these adjustments would have definite ramifications for training success, budget and staffing requirements may make such choices necessary. In any consideration of the timeline for training, we recommend that the overall Anytime, Anywhere Answers format be reviewed to determine essential elements. These can be prioritized, condensed, and organized as needed to conform to local exigencies.

CONTENT

The factors already mentioned—budget, trainers, staff, time—will lead to decisions about content. Once needed competencies have been identified, training activities can be designed that will improve skills and develop service strategies.

Libraries that wish to develop their own curriculum don't need to reinvent the wheel. The materials offered in this book and its appendixes can be tailored for local use. In addition, there are other resources that offer tools that can be incorporated into a training curriculum, with or without modification. (Note that if such materials are used, appropriate citation or other acknowledgment should be made.) As mentioned in chapter 3, Joe Barker at the University of California at Berkeley provides a tutorial on web-searching skills that is updated regularly. Debbie Flanagan's tutorial on "Web Search Strategies," also mentioned in that chapter, has exercises involving subject directories, search preparation, and more. Another good source is "Sink or Swim: Internet Search Tools and Techniques" by Ross Tyner at Okanagan University College. An extensive selection of checklists and practice exercises that simulate chat transactions, technical problems, and other online experiences are included in Anne Lipow's *The Virtual Reference Librarian's Handbook*. She also offers a sample training plan and a before, during, and after chart of activities for managers, trainers, and trainees.[1]

USABILITY

Before it is offered to learners, the curriculum should be tested to ensure that it is understandable and complete, both in written content and online design. The goals for curriculum usability are that it be useful and easy to use, that it be easy to learn and as error-free as possible, and that it be enjoyable. For virtual reference, usefulness means that the course content is up-to-date, that it reflects current service standards, and that there are measurable objectives by which to gauge training success. Ease of use relates to web design that provides consistent layout, graphic simplicity, readable text, and clear navigation. These factors, along with logical course structure and relevant assignments, contribute to making the curriculum easy to learn. Frequently checking online links will also minimize problems. Incorporating activities that involve exploring the Web, chatting online, and using real virtual reference services result in agreeable, even entertaining learning experiences.

Several different methods can be used to determine whether the curriculum lives up to these goals. First, involving developers with differing library experience and expertise means that alternate viewpoints will be heard. The staff that developed Anytime, Anywhere Answers included two public librarians with contrasting backgrounds and a library school intern. The primary developers trained on three different virtual reference software applications: LSSI, 24/7 Reference, and QuestionPoint. The Core Competencies for Virtual Reference were posted to the DIG_REF electronic discussion list and revised based on feedback. Students at the University of Washington's Information School tested web pages for usability and clarity. The URLs for the test pages were sent to experts, including Susan McGlamery (24/7 Reference), Joseph Janes (University of Washington Information School), Barbara Pitney (King County Library System), and others. The curriculum content and format were tested in a wide variety of ways. For the Secret Patron and Virtual Field Trip activities, the developers personally completed extensive testing. Parts of the content, such as Multitasking Skills and VR Policies and Procedures, were sent to librarians currently involved in virtual reference service at the King County Library

System, the University of Washington, the Metropolitan Cooperative Library System (Los Angeles), and the QandACafe (San Francisco Bay area). The content was reviewed at several stages of development by the VRS project coordinator and the Washington State Library training coordinator. There are many other methods for testing usability. Andrew K. Pace offers an excellent and thorough review of web usability in the March–April 2002 issue of *Library Technology Reports*.[2]

Although extensive measures were taken to test the curriculum's usability prior to beginning actual training, the ultimate test came from trainers and learners whose comments and suggestions led to modifications over time. (See chapter 9.) One of the primary indicators of success was the response to a question on the follow-up assessment of competencies about the percentage of course skills learned that were being used on the job. Ninety percent of respondents stated that they applied 25–100 percent of the skills they had learned to their work. No one reported using less than 10–25 percent of what they had learned.

DELIVERY

If the training will include in-person activities, it is important to provide comfortable facilities, reliable equipment, relevant software, clear and complete documentation, and refreshments. The agenda should provide a variety of activities and exercises, with well-scheduled breaks. For an example used in Anytime, Anywhere Answers, see the "Orientation" section of chapter 7.

In-person training should be offered in a computer lab equipped with up-to-date equipment and telecommunications capabilities. Old computers and slow connection speeds frustrate both trainers and learners. It is imperative that hardware and software be thoroughly tested in advance of the training date. Since many libraries are governmental institutions with tightly controlled information technology environments, it must be determined whether there are restrictions on use. For example, one portion of the VRS training orientation required that learners download a plug-in to enable instant messaging. This proved to be problematic in several situations. In one case, software that had been used without difficulty in a prior orientation at the Washington State Library computer lab created a snafu of considerable proportions when it was discovered that a new download was needed. That download in turn disabled other software used later in the day.

The VRS training orientation, titled Getting Ready for Training, began with an icebreaker activity, coffee and donuts. Two PowerPoint presentations were offered: an overview of the curriculum and a brief description and history of virtual reference. The orientation also included two hands-on exercises using different chat applications. First, pairs of learners chatted via instant messaging, then the group participated in a chat meeting using virtual reference software. The training website, projected on a screen, was used as both a guide and resource throughout the day. (See figure 1.)

For Anytime, Anywhere Answers, a binder was compiled for each learner that contained a copy of all training documents used during the orientation session. It also included dividers in which learners could place copies of other materials printed from the training website and other sources over the following weeks.

Figure 1. First Week page of the Anytime, Anywhere Answers website

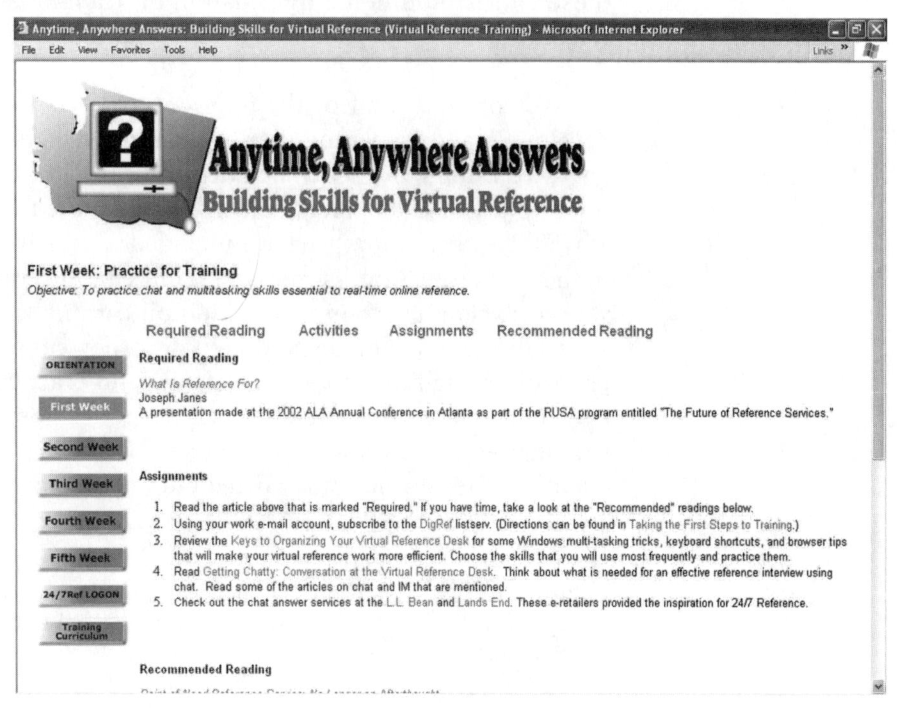

After the orientation session, learner activities were self-paced, with the exception of a scheduled chat meeting during each of the following four weeks. That meeting used a feature of the 24/7 Reference application for delivery. As it happened, our training program was the first to use many of the functions available in the chat meeting software. The software provider worked closely with training developers to ensure that the application worked reliably and to develop support documentation for continuing use. This was a separate learning experience for all involved.

Other possibilities for delivery include course management software (such as Blackboard or WebCT), videoconferencing, videotaped presentations, and online conferencing software (such as PlaceWare or WebBoard). Each of these has different strengths, weaknesses, and costs. Including a significant amount of online activity in some form is critical, since that is the environment in which virtual reference takes place. The best training incorporates a variety of delivery mechanisms that reinforce learning. A common adage is that people remember 10 percent of what they read, 20 percent of what they hear, 30 percent of what they see, 50 percent of what they both hear and see, 70 percent of what they say or write, and 90 percent of what they say while doing something.

EVALUATION

Evaluation should relate directly to training goals, measuring both success and shortcomings. Applying the results of evaluation will ensure continuing improvement in training. Chapter 9 provides a complete discussion of the assessment tools and techniques used for Anytime, Anywhere Answers, as well as the results of those efforts. Additional information on training evaluation is available at the website of the American Society for Training and Development: http://www.astd.org.

We considered all of the issues and alternatives raised in this chapter in developing and delivering the Anytime, Anywhere Answers program. In chapter 7, we will provide a detailed description of the complete curriculum used to train library staff members in Washington State from November 2002 through May 2003. In addition, we have included comments made by both learners and trainers in discussion list messages and chat meeting transcripts. These observations explain by example the kind of learning that took place in our classes. Through the assignments and activities they completed, VRS training participants discovered the kinds of behaviors and practices that they wanted to emulate or avoid when providing service to customers in their own libraries. Reading these reports is an eye-opener for anyone interested in providing high-quality service for not only virtual but any reference interaction.

NOTES

1. Ross Tyner, "Sink or Swim: Internet Search Tools and Techniques," http://www.ouc.bc.ca/libr/connect96/search.htm. Anne Lipow, *The Virtual Reference Librarian's Handbook* (New York: Neal-Schuman, 2003).
2. Andrew K. Pace, "Building and Optimizing Library Web Services," *Library Technology Reports* 38, no. 2 (March–April 2002): 1–87.

7 Learning Activities: Taking the User Perspective

A variety of activities and assignments were incorporated into the VRS curriculum to ensure that learners would experience virtual reference from the viewpoint of service users. Each activity built on those that preceded it. As mentioned in chapter 5, learners participated in a face-to-face introductory workshop, self-paced online and reading assignments, and scheduled online chat meetings. This varied format maintained interest and high participation levels for all classes. The emphasis on playing the role of customer and evaluating virtual reference services from that perspective proved invaluable, both for learners and trainers. Online discussions and posted commentaries provided a remarkable record of ideas, insights, and practical suggestions. Those results will be explored in both this chapter and the next, which examines the relationship between model reference behaviors and online reference transactions.

We will review VRS training activities here in the rough order in which they took place through the course. The training was highly interactive, a fact that affected not only the direction and quality of discussions, but also pointed toward the need for continuing adjustment. Given the combination of a service that is in relative infancy (virtual reference) and a training program that uses a new strategy (learning from the user viewpoint), this is to be expected. During one of the earliest orientation days, a trainer made an especially astute observation: "We [the trainers] are just as much learners as you [class members] are." We will also note specific changes that were implemented at the suggestion of either trainers or participants.

TRAIN THE TRAINER

In September 2002, the Anytime, Anywhere Answers curriculum was introduced to the trainers. This one and a half-day workshop took place at a Seattle Public Library computer lab. The original curriculum developers designed and delivered the workshop. Contract trainers made up most of the audience, but several observers also were present (the Statewide Virtual Reference Project coordinator, the Washington State Library training coordinator, the WSL reference program manager, and the director of the King County Law Library). Lunch was provided, and travel costs were reimbursed for trainers who came from eastern Washington. Attendance at the workshop was a requirement for contracted trainers.

The first day followed the curriculum that had been prepared for learners. The presentation took a bit longer than the actual orientation, since comments about facilitating each activity were included. The 24/7 Reference chat meeting software was demonstrated from both operator and participant sides. The benefits of pairing trainers were emphasized, including the following advantages: different perspectives are presented and explored, increased individual attention to learners, added facilitation for the meetings, and other shared duties. For each pair of trainers, one was encouraged to act as "slide pusher" while the other moderated the chat.

The second day was spent reviewing the course materials that trainers would facilitate in the distance environment. Background information about constructivist learning was provided, along with some tips for keeping learners motivated and involved during the entire five weeks. Participants were asked for their feedback on the materials, as well as ideas about how to effectively present them.

Many of the trainers felt intimidated by the sheer volume of material, wondering how they could make the many activities fit together effectively. They were told to relax, since they weren't expected to remember everything. The trainer side of the curriculum was clearly explained on the "Trainer Notes and Tips" web page (see appendix I). That page detailed each week's events and expectations and also provided sample transcripts, Secret Patron scenarios, and other assignment materials. A thorough review and discussion of those notes greatly relieved everyone. The curriculum designers assured the trainers that comfort with the content would come as a result of their experience with training. After that, they would be able to focus on delivery and facilitation skills.

Designing a training program that can be delivered by multiple trainers from varied backgrounds is a challenge. It is difficult to know how much delivery information to provide, because each trainer will have a different approach. It is also possible to overwhelm them with delivery tips before they are comfortable with the content. The VRS training program was very lucky to get both talented curriculum developers and a versatile group of trainers.

The group insisted that web pages be protected to prevent possible unauthorized use of the extensive original content. The concern focused on past experience with the use of online materials without appropriate attribution. All agreed that a minimum level of security control would be effective and that passwords should be provided to those requesting them in writing.

At the end of the Train the Trainer workshop, the developers were presented with a standing ovation of appreciation for the thoroughness and distinction of the curriculum.

ORIENTATION: GETTING READY FOR TRAINING

The orientation session mixed presentations, self-assessments, online practice, and group discussions. Trainers modified the standard agenda reproduced below in response to the skills and experience of class members, equipment problems, and other anomalies. Each class included participants from a variety of library settings, with different levels of expectation for virtual reference. Orientation sessions were held in several locations, resulting in uneven and sometimes unexpected hardware and telecommunications capabilities. These variables, along with trainer style and learner volubility, meant that sessions could end an hour early or extend beyond five o'clock. Nearby lunch possibilities also played a part—if there were none (in which case participants ate on-site), it was usually agreed to cut the lunch period short. In every case, the day ended at a mutually agreed comfort point for both trainers and learners.

One trainer developed a set of cheat sheets that offered a page of notes for each activity on the agenda. A large, bold font made the outline readable and it was shared with others for use with subsequent classes (see appendix G).

Agenda for Orientation

9:00–9:45 AM	Introductions and get-acquainted activity (Walking Billboards)
9:45–10:30 AM	Overview of training (slide presentation), syllabus, web pages
10:30–10:45 AM	Break
10:45–11:15 AM	Core competencies and initial skills assessment
11:15–Noon	Virtual Reference: A Work in Progress (slide presentation)
Noon–1:30 PM	Lunch
1:30–2:15 PM	First steps to training, instant messaging, discussion lists
2:15–2:45 PM	Answering questions using chat
2:45–3:15 PM	Tips for success, learner support, hardware/software
3:15–3:30 PM	Break
3:30–4:15 PM	Practice with online meeting software, online meeting overview
4:15–4:45 PM	Windows and Internet reference skills
4:45–5:00 PM	Wrap-up and questions

The day began with coffee and pastries, followed by a brief round of introductions. An ice-breaking exercise helped acquaint the learners with each other. The hope was that in online chat meetings and discussion list exchanges, the participants would approach the experience as friendly rather than anonymous communication. VRS training used Walking Billboards, which offered a way to share interests and begin establishing a learner community. This particular exercise was so successful that it was used in all of the 2002–03 classes.

Walking Billboards began with the group designing a get-acquainted session unique to the class. Participants were asked to suggest topics of possible mutual interest, such as hobbies, pets, favorite books, foods, ideal vacation spots, and so on. A quick vote was taken to select the five or six favorites. At that point, each participant listed their personal responses on a sheet of easel paper and taped it to his or her shoulders—hence the term "walking billboards." Then they circulated and talked, discovering conversation points and common interests. (There were a lot of travelers, shoppers, cat owners, and—no surprise—book lovers.)[1]

Following this activity, the trainers presented a slide show that outlined the curriculum over the five-week course. They described the blended learning format and training goals:

1. To facilitate the acquisition of skills
2. To support active learner participation
3. To create an ongoing learning community
4. To encourage best practices

The range of activities was reviewed. After the initial classes finished their final work, it was decided that a better explanation of the Secret Patron exercise was needed. In subsequent orientations, a sample scenario and transcript were provided to participants and the topic was discussed in greater depth. The final part of the presentation described expectations for both learners and trainers, including the commitment of time to complete assignments and online activities, the willingness to provide support, and the hope that everyone would ask questions freely and candidly.

The training syllabus was reviewed next. This required agreement on the part of both trainers and learners for scheduled online chat meetings. In the case of the early classes, this also led to a discussion of holidays and resulting conflicts. Beginning with the second round, an extra week to ten days was built into the schedule to accommodate holidays and unexpected delays.

The final part of curriculum overview was a description of the Anytime, Anywhere Answers web pages, including their organization, software requirements, and links.

Some trainers instructed class participants to not boot up their computers until after the first break. There was concern that learners would access e-mail and use other computer applications rather than focus on the class. However, it should be noted that comfort with computer multitasking is highly individual. Adult learners should be respected as able to manage class time effectively according to their personal skills and needs.

Following the morning break, core competencies were discussed. Before reviewing the official list of competencies, the class was asked to suggest the kind of aptitudes and knowledge that are required for virtual reference. A practical deliberation ensued, since learners readily identified many essential skills. Each participant then completed the "Initial Skills Assessment" (see appendix A). A second slide presentation, titled Virtual Reference: A Work in Progress, covered definitions, vendor applications, the variations and evolution of the service, and future trends. By the time that the lunch break arrived, the combination of activities and interaction had established a comfortable atmosphere for each class. This provided a good framework for the afternoon, in which learners participated in both paired and group online discussions.

The basis for chat practice described in the next section was established after lunch. In order to familiarize learners with the most common form of chat—instant messaging (IM)—participants set up an identity-neutral e-mail account with one of several different online services. They then registered for a free IM service and set up buddy lists.

This proved to be the most troublesome part of most orientation sessions, for a variety of reasons. Much time was wasted in selecting screen names, since it proved difficult to choose a moniker not already in use. Some services use a "three strikes and out" procedure, meaning that failure to successfully choose a screen name after three tries results in being booted off for twenty-four hours before another attempt is allowed. A download-free, Internet-based service was first used with minimal trouble, but later proved problematic when the software changed. The best experience resulted when a trainer set up identity-neutral accounts prior to the beginning of orientation, and learners selected from them. (Participants who previously had set up personal nicknamed accounts used them without fuss.) A chart was passed around the class on which each learner recorded their name, library, work e-mail address, identity-neutral e-mail address, and screen name for chat. This provided a written record of new names for future reference. Following this activity, which was abandoned in at least one instance due to technical obstacles, learners paired to try chatting. A set of practice questions was provided, and the sessions that followed often ended in silliness, improving the group dynamic. Humor has its place in learning!

Participants were instructed to subscribe to the DIG_REF electronic discussion list, as well as the training list set up for each VRS class. DIG_REF was recommended as essential for keeping current with the rapidly evolving world of virtual reference. The VRS training list was used for posting assignments and for keeping in touch with trainers and other learners. Recognizing the trials and errors of instant messaging, the next topic covered was Tips for Success with Online Learning. It was emphasized that along with the convenience and flexibility of e-learning comes the responsibility to manage time effectively. To achieve training success, learners were encouraged to view themselves as directing product development, and to see themselves as *the product*. Among the suggestions were:

- finding the time of day in which the individual worked best online
- breaking online sessions into smaller periods and taking time to stretch or leave the computer
- coordinating the online learning schedule with supervisors and coworkers
- working offline on written assignments prior to posting them online
- creating a schedule for deadlines to ensure that work did not fall behind
- participating actively in all activities in order to gain maximum benefit
- reflecting on what was learned from each activity, applying concepts to the local library, and sharing the conclusions on the discussion list
- sharing training experiences with coworkers to reinforce learning
- keeping in regular contact with trainers, asking questions and offering feedback, and reporting problems
- enjoying the process of learning new skills

There was additional discussion about support that learners would need and that would be offered to them, as well as the hardware and software requirements for the use of online training materials. Trainers pointed out the best configuration for using the curriculum (Windows 2000, Internet Explorer 5.0 or above, and Acrobat Reader) and also noted some problems in using Acrobat Reader with Windows XP.

The afternoon break was followed by practice with the chat meeting software, using the 24/7 Reference application. The topics for scheduled online meetings were reviewed, as were the "Norms for Online Meetings" outlined in the final section of this chapter. At this point, some participants were using online chat reference software for the first time—and it was a big hit.

Before the final wrap-up and question period, the trainers asked participants to complete the self-assessment of Windows multitasking skills and then review the Internet reference skills assessment that had been completed prior to arriving at orientation. (See appendix A for copies of these tools.) Tips for efficient use of the desktop and methods for upgrading skills were offered to learners who identified areas of need (see appendix G).

In every class, the day ended with an expression of appreciation on the part of the learners for both the trainers' skills and the training activities. Each class was unique, but all were enjoyable. The face-to-face orientation established common ground at the very beginning of training, one which provided much-needed rapport for the following weeks.

CHAT PRACTICE

The importance of understanding chat culture was discussed at the orientation, citing the prevalent use of this technique by teenagers. Since teens are potential lifelong library patrons and many are also avid online users, a knowledge of chat lingo and practices was seen as critical. Students logging on to a virtual reference service may use the same abbreviations and icons they employ in casual online chat, and library operators should be able to interpret their meaning. A Pew Study of teen behavior on the Internet found that the anonymity of chat appears to reduce inhibitions, and users seem more likely to say something in a chat room that they would not say in person. The second week included reading "Getting Chatty: Conversation at the Virtual Reference Desk," which introduced chat methods, tips, and concepts (see appendix G).

In addition to the chat practice incorporated into the orientation session, learners were encouraged to use instant messaging at work and home, if possible. A number of learners reported that they already were frequent users of IM and regarded that as an advantage for virtual reference service. Apart from understanding common protocols that have developed in online chat rooms and in IM use, practice with chat helps establish habits that are important to virtual reference. Keeping exchanges brief, ignoring misspellings and punctuation, and learning patience while waiting for a response are all approaches that make virtual reference transactions effective.

Until the last round of 2003 classes, an instant messaging application also was used for the first of the four scheduled online weekly meetings. This had mixed reviews, and when problems were encountered with application software changes, this format was eliminated for the final classes. Nonetheless, both curriculum developers and trainers felt that there was significant value in exposing virtual reference operators to instant messaging. We are exploring alternative ways to provide this practice in future classes, including a search for download-free applications.

MULTITASKING SKILLS

Few skills needed in virtual reference are as daunting as multitasking. Younger practitioners who have grown up with computers and the Internet may be more adept in handling several concurrent tasks or customers. They readily read e-mail, listen to music, send instant messages, and search the Internet simultaneously. Unfortunately, not all library staff members have either the youth or the flexibility that this requires. It helps to envision work on the traditional public service desk, where many different tasks may take place at the same time: answering the telephone, helping a customer, recording statistics, photocopying, and so on. Such activities are not always conveniently timed so that staff can concentrate on a single one. In the case of virtual reference, several scenarios can be imagined. While it is recommended that virtual reference work be carried out in a private room or secluded area, staffing constraints may make it necessary to provide service at the public desk. This means that in-person customers and telephone calls may arrive at the same time that an operator is involved in an online reference transaction. This is as much multitasking as is the handling of multiple, simultaneous virtual reference sessions.

There is no substitute for practice to improve the skills needed to handle such situations effectively. However, VRS training did provide both a self-assessment tool ("Windows Multitasking Competencies," appendix A) for participants to use in judging their skills and also tips and techniques to improve their use of Windows ("Keys to Organizing Your Virtual Reference Desk," appendix G).

VIRTUAL FIELD TRIPS

The first online activity required of participants was Virtual Field Trips, in which they explored a variety of library websites that offered virtual reference service. While most learners chose to visit the sites of libraries like those in which they worked, they were encouraged to review others (e.g., both academic and public ones). To prepare for the activity, they were instructed to read "The Great Reference Debate," an article about the future of traditional reference librarians. They were then asked to consider the validity of the visions offered in the article, including the question "Are reference librarians toast?"[2]

Learners were also asked to read the focus group results reported by the Statewide Virtual Reference Project.[3] It was recommended that particular attention be paid to the users' comments about not knowing what services or resources to expect from a library, along with the comment about not wanting to feel stupid when using the library or being helped by staff. This was an ideal starting point for thinking about virtual reference from the customers' perspectives.

The objective of Virtual Field Trips was to explore various library websites and then answer a series of questions about them ("Virtual Field Trip Questions," appendix C). Although the participants could—and some did—ask a real-time question during the field trip, it was noted that the reference transaction was actually part of the separate Secret Patron activity scheduled for the following week. The field trip exercise explored virtual reference services from five perspectives:

- branding
- accessiblity
- scope of service
- authority
- privacy and data gathered

The assignment instructions were to:

> Select three websites to visit from the "Virtual Reference Service Sites Grid" (see figure 2), choosing a variety of service types (public, academic, other). Note the hours of availability for each service.
>
> Print copies of the Virtual Field Trip questions, one for each site visited. Use these questions to evaluate the sites.
>
> Summarize impressions and post them to the VRS training discussion list. Which sites would serve as good examples for planning and implementing the learner's own virtual reference service?

The grid of sites included more than four dozen multitype libraries across the United States, Canada, and the United Kingdom. The services offered (chat, e-mail) and the chat vendor application used were listed for each library. A direct link to each library website was provided from the grid. Maintaining this grid was a labor-intensive effort for the project coordinator, given changing URLs, hours of service, and similar data. Learners and trainers were requested to report broken links and other problems.

Participants were given a list of considerations to use in writing summaries after recording their impressions of site visits:

- What were your overall impressions, as a patron, of the sites that you visited?
- Which of the three sites did you think was the most user-friendly? Least user-friendly? Why?

Figure 2. "Virtual Reference Service Sites Grid"

Virtual Reference Service Sites - Microsoft Internet Explorer

File Edit View Favorites Tools Help

VIRTUAL REFERENCE SERVICE SITES GRID

Virtual Reference Service Sites	Services Offered		Chat Service Software	Access Restrictions
Public Libraries	Email	Chat		
Alhambra Public Library	X	X	24/7 Reference	None
Anaheim Public Library		X	24/7 Reference	None
Arlington Heights Memorial Library North Suburban Library System		X	Virtual Reference Software (LSSI)	None
Baltimore County Public Library	X	X	Virtual Reference Software (LSSI)	None
Boston Public Library	X	X	24/7 Reference	None
Cleveland Public Library CLEVNET Library Consortium	X	X	Virtual Reference Software (LSSI)	Zip Code CPL 44114
Denver Public Library	X	X	Virtual Reference Software (LSSI)	None
East Hampton Library Suffolk County Cooperative Library System	X	X	LivePerson	None
Enoch Pratt Free Library	X	X	QuestionPoint	None
Gateshead Libraries	X	X	Click & Care	None
Harford County Public Library		X	Virtual Reference Software (LSSI)	None
King County Library System	X	X	Virtual Reference Software (LSSI)	None
Memorial Hall Library	X	X	24/7 Reference	None
Montgomery County Public Libraries	X	X	LiveAssistance	None
Morley Library NOLA Regional Library System	X	X	eShare NetAgent	Library Card D1AAA

- What positive feedback would you give to the staff who designed the sites? What improvements would you suggest?
- As a patron, did you discover anything new or unexpected?
- What did you observe that you want to remember in planning and implementing your own virtual reference service?

The critiques posted to the online training discussion list, along with reactions and commentaries from trainers and other learners, were detailed and honest. They also demonstrated the varying expectations of individual learners. The trip reports ranged from single paragraphs to several pages in length. There was concern that those who prepared long messages would not be able to sustain such a work level—and quantity was not the original intent of the curriculum developers. Trainers were prompted to advise that it was not necessary to detail every aspect of every website, but rather to summarize general impressions and describe any exceptional attributes, good or bad.

For each class, this initial exercise resulted in both practical and thought-provoking observations. Some of the most thoughtful postings are reproduced here. (The comments have been edited for readability and to remove institutional and individual identities.)

Branding

> "I was surprised to see that the large academic libraries had not done a better job of branding their services and putting this information in a prominent location on web pages throughout their sites. This reinforces my belief that my library needs to work on this issue and place our logo throughout our website."

> "As a patron I was surprised at how little was done to advertise the availability of VR services. Had I not known they were available, I would not have spent time looking for them. The lack of eye-catching logos or links made me wonder if the libraries are perhaps not ready or equipped for a high volume of VR users."

> "Overall, all sites needed more 'punch' if they really want to attract patron use—and that's an issue, I think. Some sites seem to be unsure just how much service they want to offer. It was as if they said to themselves, 'Well, everyone else is doing it, so we'd better,' but had no real sense of why or any real support behind it. This can be deadly if the service just sits there like a 300-pound gorilla and never gets off the ground, but just quietly goes away. Administrators need to commit and then market, market, market."

> "What the heck was [Private University] library thinking when it developed their 'virtual reference' icon? . . . . It looks like it came from two different clip-art programs and is supremely ugly. On the plus side, though, it's really hard to miss on the library home page—the eye is drawn to it and cannot look away. Ugh!"

> "As I see how individual libraries brand their services, I keep thinking about how virtual reference service is being branded nationwide as

something that users may come to expect when they visit library websites. So many new services have popped up that users who use multiple libraries now see it at the various libraries they visit. Because of this, I kind of like the idea of naming them similarly, such as Ask-a-Librarian. At the same time, as we tailor our services to our own user populations, it makes sense to create these services with individual identities."

Accessibility

"While I was checking out various services, I couldn't help but notice libraries' overall web presence. Some pages are great, many are fine, some are kind of awful. If the web page itself isn't friendly, usable, helpful, easy to navigate, then the virtual reference service's appeal and credibility may suffer. Now that we're spending considerable time and effort developing services for our users as they work off-site, we've got to devote just as much attention to designing usable, accessible, helpful websites. In fact, libraries' websites should probably be shining examples of usability; too often they're just a jumble of links and graphics. If our websites are confusing and difficult to navigate, we'll push our users away."

"[Public University Library] 'Real Help! Right Now! Click Here!'—That's great, but the service was actually hard to find."

"I visited three public libraries before I remembered to visit an academic one. . . . No library had accessibility to chat in more than two spots on the website and none of them on the catalog page. I like the logo and term—ASK US! at [Private University] better than the public libraries. It was easy to spot on the main page and was jargon free. [Large Public Library] used the logo KnowItNow24X7 which seems too 'jargon' for the average user to recognize. [Medium Public Library] uses its library logo (with 'Chat Live Ask a Librarian' around it) and the logo overshadowed the chat aspect so much I didn't notice it at first glance. This library was the only one that had the logo in two useful places (main and youth pages). The worst was [Medium Public Library], which embedded chat under Online Services . . . click to Got A Question? which then linked to an e-mail and chat page."

"The only presence on the home page is a test link: 'Need Help? Ask A Librarian,' along with another 'Ask a Librarian' button at the bottom of the page. Clicking on the Ask A Librarian link takes you to the 'Ask A Librarian' page. . . . From the Ask A Librarian page, you can choose to 'Chat Online—Live,' which takes you to (yet) another page, 'E-mail your reference question,' which takes you to (yet) another page with a reference form, or the instruction to 'Phone the reference desk' which provides a phone number and a link to the library hours. When you (finally) arrive at the page where you can actually initiate a chat session, the only information provided beyond the button 'Chat Live with a Librarian Now!' is text below: 'Live chat for General Reference is typically available, when classes are in session, between 9:00 am and 10:00 pm, with limited hours on weekends.' And if you like circular navigation, you can click on the Ask A Librarian button that appears (again) at the bottom of the screen and start the cycle all over again! It does appear that the button bar that includes 'Ask A Librarian' is part of a standard footer that shows up at the bottom of screens that seem to be part of the local website. However, it is not present once you enter the library catalog, so at best, you are always three clicks away from VR, and once you are in the catalog, at least four clicks. *If* you can keep track of the correct navigation. Along with this, you will always lose your place unless you remember to open a new browser window to initiate your trip down the path to VR. As a side note, the home icon that appears with the toolbar buttons at the bottom of the page takes you to the [Large Private University] home page, *not* the library home page, which seems out of context with the rest of the toolbar buttons. There are no stated restrictions on and/or requirements for VR service. The wording in the statement 'typically available, when classes are in session' does imply that VR, even during operating hours, may not always be available. Once you click on the 'Chat Live with a Librarian Now!' button, a pop-up window asks for your [university status] classification. The ID on this pop-up window is 'Groopz,' although the VRS grid indicates their service as 'Desktop Streaming.' My VR page was ignored (because I indicated I was an outsider?), so the button defaults to a link to the Ask A Librarian e-mail form page."

Trainer's comment to above posting

"What a confusing site to navigate. Was the overall library's web page as confusing? It's amazing how we can learn to work around 'circular' flaws."

Learner's reply

"Other navigation errors are long pages without any page navigation (top/bottom) and no way to 'back out' of the catalog (using browser navigation). You *have* to select the 'Libraries Home' link to get back to their main page, or pick an item from the pull-down menu list that breaks you out of the catalog page. They also offer a Virtual Reference Desk which has nothing to do with VR service as we know it, but is more like a combination of ready reference/FAQs/online resources. At least the Ask a Librarian link is available from these pages. . . . I realize that many of these things may be or seem trivial, but as a long-time user interface and website developer, I know they are little glitches that impede effective navigation and use of a site (just like long page-load times!). Often they give users a negative feeling about the system/site."

Scope of Service

"[State College Library] did not provide any information about the kinds of questions best suited to their live chat service, but they did provide a link to a tutorial for students needing help with the research process."

"There is a disclaimer about legal and medical advice and a note that extensive genealogical questions cannot be answered. The service is appropriate for 'questions that can be answered quickly and effectively using online resources.' There are two links—'Ask a Reference Question' and 'Ask a Homework Question.' One makes the assumption that the Homework chat is answered by a youth services librarian and the Reference chat by a regular reference librarian, but that is not stated anywhere."

"The real-time virtual reference service falls into the general services of the Undergraduate Library. This means that the FAQ topics for the services would show it on a list of services for undergraduates, such as 'research for a paper' and 'using electronic resources at home.' The service is a quick-answer service; to my mind, no research help is available (one remembers there are 40,000 students). . . . Two limitations on the service are (1) that it is limited to brief, factual, ready-reference questions and (2) that questions should take around 15 minutes to answer."

Authority

"I wasn't able to figure out who provided 'Ask a Librarian' reference services. Having staffed the main reference desk twenty years ago as a student, I know that library school students may staff the service. I had two impressions: (1) that the [Large Public University] affiliation was authority enough (it didn't matter what the credentials were of the folks doing it) and (2) any bright person could staff the service and offer quick answers."

"Other than the generic referrals to 'reference services,' there is no indication of who might be providing VR services. The e-mail reference form . . . does say that the question is sent to a reference librarian. I didn't spot any disclaimers about advice provided, copyright restrictions, or citing online sources (not even on their homework resources page)."

"The service information page explains that staff includes local reference librarians, reference librarians from the [Large Urban Public Cooperative], and graduate library school students. There are no other statements regarding qualifications or subject expertise. There are no medical or legal disclaimers, copyright statements, or guidelines about citing online resources."

Confidentiality and Data Gathered

"A link to the privacy/confidentiality statement is prominently positioned on the service information page. The privacy statement . . . is extensive and thorough. Information retained is e-mail address and a cookie for accessing some functions. There is a contract provided if the patron wishes to have deleted any link to personal information on the server."

"I find myself looking more for links to privacy policies and personal data retention statements—it was a bit of a shock to me when I found out my library's chat service software collects the IP addresses of participants. Now I look to see if other services say anything about that. . . . For many people this address is traceable to their own personal computer. None of the sites I visited get particularly high marks in this, but I think [National Library] comes off best. There was no information (that I saw) on privacy or personal data on chat service forms, but the Ask a Librarian form (the one that is submitted to their e-mail service) has a link to a very clear privacy policy, which includes information on cookies. . . . [Private University], on the other hand, buried its privacy policy something like three links past the form, on the policy page of the [Collaborative Reference Service]. The [Collaborative Service] policy states that 'we will not disclose any personal data we collect from you to any other party in a manner that would identify you, except where required by law or in order to fulfill your service request. Data will be deleted annually,' unless the user checks a box indicating that they prefer anonymity. In that case, personal data is erased before archiving."

Example of a Trainer's Summary of Virtual Field Trip Reports

"Hi all!

The Virtual Field Trip proved to be just as much fun as it was interesting, and it looks like you all discovered some valuable insights while doing so.

In reading the assignment summaries, we noted that having a suitable name for the VR service was quite important: for example, the logo/branding of the [Large Public Library] was not really appreciated by anyone. Having a logo that is somewhat demeaning and juvenile (as was pointed out by two of you) seems to defeat the purpose of a library being a learning environment. We remember hearing a discussion of VR logos at ALA Annual Conference last year; some libraries had changed theirs multiple times in an effort to find one that worked.

Some other interesting insights we noted in reading the assignments:

Several of you mentioned that having an appealing logo and sites that are easy to navigate are important issues when setting up the services. We like the statement that [County Library] was "simple yet attractive." This is essential for building clientele, so to speak. It was also mentioned that the [Private University Library] site took a long time to load because of all the graphics and tables. In my mind it all goes back to the line in *Field of Dreams:* 'If you build it they will come,' but then how long will they be willing to wait? Are people going to want to wait for this type of library service to load, or are they going to get impatient and move on to Ask Jeeves and Ask Google instead? Will they chalk it up to the library trying to drum up more business and essentially going overboard with taxpayer dollars? Keeping it simple is a very good thing indeed, in my opinion.

We also found it quite interesting that you all noted that there was a difference in the marketing/branding of the public vs. the academic libraries. It was pointed out that academic library sites often were much more 'texty.' Another comment was that privacy statements are dull to read, but this is a pretty important aspect to include. Perhaps including this information on a linked second page would be better? That way the information is there, but not 'clogging up' the front-line pages as much. As noted, some sites were missing privacy policies entirely. Everyone seemed to point out in some form or other that having the different subjects of the pages laid out in topical groupings, and even offering different buttons leading to the various groupings, was handy. Having these items grouped in bullet format was seen as even more convenient.

In regard to layout, everyone also seemed to note in one way or another that navigating through the sites and finding links to the service on all pages was important. Also keeping pages consistent (especially fonts) was important. All in all, most of the logos/branding needed to be a bit 'flashier' or 'jazzier.' Several of you mentioned compliance with ADA standards also.

One participant noted the value of having links to information about 'netiquette' and rules of conduct; other content information came up as well. The comment about the value of the [Cooperative Virtual Reference Service] being able to provide legal and medical information showcases one of the many advantages of a consortial system that pulls from a wide variety of libraries.

You all did a great job on the assignment, and we are sure you picked up a few tips for your own services and pages to make them even more effective and user-friendly."

The preceding samples of postings from an extensive archive illustrate the range and nature of learners' opinions. Among their many conclusions were that:

Libraries tend to provide inconsistent and often unmemorable branding of virtual reference services, while the best services were easy to find (eye-catching, no need to scroll in order to locate, clearly and consistently branded).

Websites that invited customers to return were uncluttered, used easy-to-read fonts, were jargon-free, and were sparing in the use of text.

Good services also were easy to use, navigate, and understand—the service should be clearly described. Unfortunately, libraries more often than not make it difficult to access the virtual reference service by burying links several pages deep, offering very limited service hours, and using a variety of terms to refer to the same service.

In many cases, service is limited by length of time or the nature of questions, which would be difficult for a customer to define (what is "quick" or "ready reference"?).

Rarely do libraries indicate the qualifications of those who will provide answers to customer questions. Libraries should provide a clear authority statement.

There seems to be an all-or-nothing approach to privacy statements—either extensive, thorough statements are provided or none at all. Libraries should provide prominent links to privacy and confidentiality statements.

There is a rich archive of experience contained in the first year of the VRS training discussion list comments, and we expect that more germane and useful perceptions will result from future training sessions.

SECRET PATRON

For developers, trainers, and learners alike, no training activity offered greater insight into the heart of virtual reference service than the Secret Patron exercise. As its name implies, the activity involves anonymous visits to virtual reference services, followed by a careful evaluation of the interaction. This is not a new idea. The "secret shopper" approach has been used for decades to assess customer service in the retail sector. The same approach is part of the evaluation of Effective Reference Performance training as designed by Transform, Inc. The University of Maryland's College of Information Studies also evaluated VR research using an approach termed "unobtrusive observer."

Secret Patron focuses on the myriad ways in which our customers ask questions. It is no secret that we are often bewildered or exasperated by the user's approach to finding information. What seems logical and straightforward to the patron is arcane or convoluted to the librarian. In observing library staff members practicing virtual reference with each other, it was noted that they ask questions in ways that make sense to themselves and to other librarians. The curriculum developers felt strongly that real patron queries should be used in this role-playing, complete with their awkwardness and confusion. This activity explored the effectiveness of the chat reference interview in clarifying the user's query.

In early VRS training classes, a few learners expressed varying degrees of discomfort with the Secret Patron approach. They worried about using other libraries' staff time for training purposes, expressed uneasiness with the implied deception, and voiced other similar concerns. One learner assuaged his guilt by identifying himself and his purpose to the virtual reference operator at the end of the Secret Patron exercise. In answer to these declared concerns, several modifications were employed. A sample scenario and the transcript from which it was developed were included in the orientation package. This provided a basis for discussing the exercise and explaining the merit of using actual patron questions, with their accompanying context (age, experience with the Internet, attitude, research skills, etc.). Among other things, it was noted that virtual reference operators often invite staff members from other libraries to test their service, as a demonstration of both the whiz-bang! factor and usefulness. This eased some learners' doubts. Trainers were encouraged to respect and honor the learners as adults who were able to articulate their personal needs. So when questions arose, they explored alternative ways in which to structure the activity. Some learners formulated their own scenarios. Trainers reiterated the goal of emulating the customer's viewpoint and suggested ways in which to make the questions more user-focused or more challenging. One of the more interesting scenarios is reproduced here.

Learner Scenario for Public Library

You are:

A fourth grader who is concerned about conversations between her parents that she has overheard. She is looking for personal information about divorce.

Your approach to asking a question is:

Hesitant and vague, with typical spelling errors and the limited vocabulary of a fourth grader. You are very interested in the way the librarian responds to you.

You start with:

i want to know about divorce

Then you say:

i heard my mom say unreckognisable diference and i don't know what this means

The majority of learners used scenarios provided in the curriculum and assigned by trainers. Each learner was given a specific role to use with three different services. They then chose libraries from the "Virtual Reference Service Sites Grid," matching the question to an appropriate type of library. After the first four classes had completed work, a new set of scenarios was developed (each batch included about two dozen different roles and questions). There was concern that an individual library might be pelted with reiterations of the same question.

Anonymity allows candor. The VRS training participants experienced dubious service more often than good, and their discussion list messages were openly critical. Here is an example, written by a municipal public library reference manager:

"Sneaky Patron Strikes Out"

> "I was using Scenario 14, trying to find a self-help book written in the early '90s by the person who created Microsoft Word and then left Microsoft (with follow-up information that the author's first name was Richard). What an eye opener!
>
> The operator at [Urban Public Library 1] was the only one of three that adopted a welcoming, friendly 'chat' personality and was careful to address me all the time by my name. However, from the very start, he was convinced I was thinking of a novel called *Microserf* (I

> think) by Douglas someone and couldn't get off that line of thinking, even when I said I thought the first name started with an R (I even suggested Richard, Rick, Robert). He explained searching Google but said he couldn't come up with anything close to what I was describing. He showed me a summary of the novel from their catalog but didn't suggest any other avenue when I wasn't satisfied. I asked if he could work a little more on it and get back to me later, and he said he'd do that. (The funny thing is, after the call, I did a quick search on Google and found it right away.)
>
> Well, on to [Urban Public Library 2], which was even more bizarre. The first operator, without any reference interview, transferred me to the Social Sciences Department, where all of a sudden I was seeing a conversation between two staff members about some arcane reference transaction not related to me at all. Finally, once they were paying attention to me, their first response was to present me with a list of about 50 authors and ask me if it was any of them. I said no, gave my 'Richard' follow-up (there was no reference interview), and waited a very long time. Finally the librarian said she was checking a history of Microsoft. I waited another long time. Then she said the only person she could turn up was Bill Gates but that he had not left the company. By this time I was writhing in pain on the floor. I asked if they could work on it some more, and they said they would.
>
> [County Library] was pretty much the same story—a little friendlier and more personable than [Urban Public Library 2]. There still was no reference interview—I finally had to offer the 'Richard' follow-up. This site was the worst for extraordinarily long silences with no indication to me of what was happening. The only way I could get any response was to send a message asking 'How's it going?' They couldn't turn up anything. During the final long silence I told them that I had found the answer on Google. They said something like, 'Oh, that's good. Please call us if you have any more questions.' Right.
>
> Otherwise I had a pretty good day. If librarians don't have anything more than this to offer in competition with Google and the likes, I'll stick with the big 'G.'"

This was a frequently irritating or frustrating experience for learners, although certainly there were bright online moments. Much was surprising, and some unfortunate themes developed, from the failure to offer the waiting customer feedback to the lack of question clarification. There is no doubt that VRS training participants discovered preferred online practices as well as examples of poor service. It is also possible that library staff members were more critical of service than customers would be, but that should not excuse questionable, abbreviated, or unprofessional practices.

Because the Secret Patron exercise was directly related to model reference behaviors, a more extensive examination of learner experiences will be detailed in chapter 8. It is worth noting here that nearly all the participants found this activity both informative and stimulating. On the "Evaluation of Training" form, these were typical responses to the question, "In this training, what was most beneficial to you?"

"I found the Secret Patron exercise to be most enlightening!"

"Exercises—especially secret patron and reviewing transcripts, and then thinking about and reporting back to the group."

"Seeing what other libraries' websites looked like and critiquing them, and going on and asking a question in our Secret Patron assignment. The librarians who answered my question were quick and very knowledgeable."

TRANSCRIPT REVIEW

For the fourth week exercise, trainers e-mailed copies of several chat reference transcripts (see appendix B) to learners. Alternatively, transcripts from Secret Patron activities could be used. In either case, the participants were instructed to read and then comment on the transactions, keeping in mind the Reference and User Services Association's reference guidelines. A list of questions was provided as an aid to framing their observations, focusing on different aspects of the service provided:

- overall impressions
- rating and explaining effectiveness
- feedback and improvements for service providers
- information literacy instruction
- behaviors and practices that could be emulated
- ways in which to use transcripts as tools for service improvement

Like the Secret Patron exercise, this activity focused on the quality of service offered to customers. The transcripts were selected to reflect a variety of factors that affected that quality in both public and academic library settings. Helping with homework, citing sources, suggesting multiple relevant resources and print materials, offering opinions, and clarifying the question were all illustrated with varying degrees of success. Quotes from some learner commentaries follow.

Overall Impressions

"The service seemed to be very abbreviated and even rushed at times. In some cases the librarians were able to quickly find some relevant information, but it seemed that they didn't really get to the meat of the research question. Obviously even reference interviews in person sometimes don't quite get to the heart of the matter, but perhaps visual cues in the patron's body language help us know if we're getting what they need."

"I can find something good about each one that possibly I should be doing and am not. There are also some things I would not do. For example, I think the librarian should address the person by name and say 'Hello, whoever, I'm the librarian' and go from there to whether the question needs to be clarified. All of the transcripts except example 5 started out with 'Please hold' or some such statement instead of addressing the patron or introducing the librarian."

"The librarians in the transcripts seemed rushed, less than thorough, although we don't have exact timelines so it's hard to be sure. No one asked how soon the patron needed the info, although that may have come with the question on the chat form. All wanted to push websites, with one exception. . . . Looking for articles can also be extremely time consuming, especially since each one has to be examined by the librarian and user for viability. We continue to return to the issue of speed vs. accuracy, perceived wants vs. actual needs, format vs. utility, etc."

Effectiveness

"Of the transactions provided, I found example 5 to be the most effective. The librarian asked a clarifying question, recommended a resource, and offered to show the patron how to find and get the book even though her library didn't own it."

"Example 2 was somewhat weaker for a couple reasons. First, the librarian provided an answer to the patron's question but did not provide a source for the information until the patron asked for one. Even then, what was provided was not a definite citation. . . . Then the librarian closed the session before the patron did, and the patron tried to ask for more information. This was a good example of why a librarian should wait for the patron to sign off first."

Feedback and Improvements

"I liked the little moments of friendly interaction such as 'Tough question!' or 'good luck!'"

"Transcripts of chat sessions are absorbing reading. . . . I believe the comment from last week's secret patron activity about the value of spontaneous comments versus scripts is borne out by these documents; it is clear to see which is which, and the scripts do sound stiff and unwelcoming."

"A difficult situation to be in would be having an impatient patron when you are having difficulty finding the answer, as in number 6. One of the mistakes this librarian made was to start pushing pages before she found the answer. . . . Offering to e-mail the answer was probably a good strategy in this situation."

Information Literacy Instruction

"Again, I learn from example 3 to respect the patron's decision to search no more. The closing was good in asking if there was anything else needed. I do think this librarian may have missed a chance for information literacy. She could have addressed the patron's debate and made it clear to locate sources that support each side of the argument and also to use evaluation criteria to decide what to use on the Web or in print."

"I think there were opportunities for literacy instruction in all of these transcripts. Any time you are leading the patron to information, there is the opportunity to at least describe (some of) the searching process that is taking place."

Best Practices

"What do I want to remember—probe, probe, probe, clarify the question!"

"Example 6. Wow. Talk about going the extra mile!"

"Remember: Watch the tendency to be satisfied with the first source found; give the patron time to respond; give the patron time to really look at web pages before asking if the answer is ok; think about how literacy training would fit in a particular situation."

"In a true evaluation of this reference encounter, I'd be interested in knowing how the patron rated it and if he/she would be interested in using the service again."

Transcripts as Tools for Improvement

"Speaking of instruction, having transcripts and e-mail responses available for viewing is a great teaching tool for me. We have not had many chat transcripts to view, but we do have a number of e-mail responses. . . . I try to review them at least once a week, seeing how someone gave a courteous, well-thought-out answer to a patron's question, picking up tips along the way. Even, once in a while, patting myself on the back for doing a decent job of my own."

"I think our group, especially those within our own library system, should share some of our transcript questions and find out from each other how he/she went about answering and what websites or databases were used. This may help all of us when a similar question is asked."

"These kinds of transcripts can help identify training issues (is there an area we need to brush up on?), staffing issues (do we have enough staff to do this right?), work space issues (do we need more ready reference sources available where the librarians work?), and technology issues (do we really have the tools to do this right?). Without identifying participants, sample transcripts could be posted on the library's Intranet or in print training manuals to demonstrate issues to staff."

"I hope I can be as ruthless with myself as I was with these transcripts when I start looking at my own."

Trainer's Comments on Transcript Assignment

"Evaluating transcripts can be a little intimidating and embarrassing. No one likes to look at themselves and critique their own work, just like we don't like to see ourselves on that little video camera at the bank or listen to our own messages on voice mail! But it is a valuable learning tool and a new one that has arisen with this new technology. One note was that it was 'almost like having a videotape of your reference interview.'

Everyone thought that the 'Hawaiian Shirt' example was the most effective interaction, and the 'Moses' question consistently came up as not the kind of service we like to see. The librarian there even closed the session before the patron was done. You have to wonder if that librarian ever looked at that transcript and if so, how he or she felt about that. There were many other examples given of good and bad practices. Everyone liked the ones where the librarian was responsive and friendly. One thing that came up consistently was the lack of incorporating an instruction/information literacy component. There were many ignored opportunities for that 'teachable moment.' A number of you also noted that there was a little too much 'on the Web' and not enough 'in the Library.'

In regard to the interesting comment about evaluating websites—this would be an excellent tip to pass on to our patrons. We want to make sure they know how to get to the authoritative sites by demonstrating, not just pushing pages too quickly, but then also making sure the patrons know how to choose one site over another.

Several pointed out that the reference interview is another important issue to remember: we need to clarify the question, and grade level if necessary, and teach as we go. Ask the all-important follow-up questions. A number of you really focused on the reference interview aspects (or lack of them).

We were reminded that the kinds of services libraries are offering now with digital reference are extremely new to our patrons, as they are to us, so professionalism is extremely important. One of the things we really saw in the value of transcripts was a way to assess tone. We may not be able to hear an aural tone, but vibes come across loud and clear by reading transcripts.

Transcript evaluation is something we as reference librarians have never had access to before. There is sometimes a perception that there is an unwritten rule of making suggestions to other librarians about reference desk interactions, but this moves beyond that limitation (of course, it shouldn't be used in a punitive manner). We can learn from our and each other's mistakes; but even better, we can be inspired by seeing transactions that show excellent professionalism, service techniques, and quality reference work."

These reports illustrate the usefulness of transcripts as a means for reinforcing effective virtual reference service. Until the advent of chat-based reference, the transaction was ephemeral. If technology evolves (as expected) to include voice and video capabilities, it may become ephemeral again—or at least, until transcripts of oral transactions are available. We have a window of opportunity to test our ideal of traditional, in-person service against the recorded interaction with customers.

CHECKING OUT THE COMPETITION

Another fourth week activity led learners to two commercial web-based question-answering services that charge fees. Google Answers (http://answers.google.com) and AskEarth (http://askearth.com/go/home) provide distinctive contrasts to library chat reference. Two readings were provided as background for this activity: "Paying for Answers Online" by Ben Arnoldy, and Tara Calishain's "New Google Answers Service Raises a Few Questions of Its Own" (see the bibliography for complete citations).

Learners were instructed to read the Google Answers FAQ (Frequently Asked Questions), and also to note the qualifications of the researchers who provide information, the pricing structure, privacy policy, and related issues. On returning to the main page, they searched on a question ("Are string beans kosher?") in the "Answered Questions" category and examined the answers. The sources used to answer the question were noted, as well as the variety of comments. Participants checked the Google Answers Terms of Service for disclaimers and limits on liability. Finally, they reviewed the Researcher Training Manual to determine service expectations, noting the emphasis on providing the search strategy used in finding answers.

Learners also checked AskEarth, a similar answer-for-fee service based in southern California. Questions that have been asked and/or answered are listed in browsing categories. The service relies on a community of people who have registered to answer questions in topical areas and are alerted to new queries.

Although they were not assigned to post observations on this activity to the discussion list, both trainers and learners did comment either on the list or in chat meetings. They noted that while digital reference is an extension of traditional library reference service, the commercial question-answering services that were reviewed for this assignment offered little evidence of:

- customer service orientation
- researchers' ability to determine user needs
- researchers' ability to use multiple sources
- researchers' ability to evaluate resources
- providing instruction in information literacy
- creating web guide sites and directories

The fees offered to answer some questions astonished some: "$30 to find the source of an Alfred Hitchcock quotation? $200 for the name of the lowest taxed city or county in Kentucky? To think we do it for free!"

POLICY AND PROCEDURE REVIEW

The final activity in each class was an exploration of libraries' virtual reference policies and procedures posted online. Using another grid of links to more than three dozen library virtual reference services, participants chose three examples each from three categories: Service Overview for Users, Examples of Privacy Statements, and Guidelines for Staff. The grid identified both library type (public/academic) and services offered (chat/e-mail) for each link. Such policies and procedures form the foundation for service, and the previous weeks' activities provided a background for analyzing them. Learners summarized their impressions after considering a series of questions that examined aspects of these documents (appendix E):

- setting up the service
- scope of service
- evaluation
- virtual collections
- referral of questions and follow-up
- staffing
- hours of availability
- databases and document delivery
- administration
- confidentiality
- patron conduct

Learners were encouraged to bookmark any examples that would be helpful in developing policies and procedures for their local service. Overall, this was a positive experience, since a number of examples of excellent guidelines for service were found. Participants from an early class reported that after completing the training, they modified an existing policy for local virtual reference service based on what they learned in this exercise.

Some excerpts from learners' postings follow.

Service Overview

> "[State University] I liked this one because it was clearly written and uncluttered. I also like that it encouraged students to use the reference desk. In the e-mail reference guidelines, I thought giving examples of typical questions was useful."

> "[Municipal Public Library] Guidelines too long and wordy; not very inviting, too many rules. My reaction would be: Why bother? They're really not interested in helping me out."

> "[State University] Very specific, well-formatted, easy-to-read page. Addresses what they will and will not provide and where to go if your question is outside the scope of this service, an excellent idea. Addresses time frame and inappropriate behavior."

> "On this score, the [National Service] was the best, hands down! I very much enjoyed the attractive and uncluttered layout; they used lots of white space with a good mix of text and graphics, with a nice friendly font and pastels that were, on the whole, inviting."

> "I only visited academic sites this time. The first sites I visited presented a policy that violates my understanding of the professionalism of service expected from libraries. [Private College] and [Large Public University] clearly state that remote users are less important than 'in-person' users.

As a patron at the college, where this is the first 'service' listed, I would immediately go somewhere else."

Privacy Statements

"[University Library] spells out their privacy policy rather clearly, explaining that no one but library staff has access to personal information. They apparently have no policy of stripping personal data after a certain period, or if they do, they don't say so. Their statement may have sufficed a year ago, but now more and more users want to know exactly what we know about them, how long we keep that info, and under what circumstances it could be shared with or without their consent. [University Library] states on their page 'Every effort will be made to protect your privacy. However, you should always use good judgment about discussing personal or private matters by e-mail.' Eeeek!"

"I went to [College Library Cooperative], [Public Library Cooperative], and [Provincial Library]. First let me point out that I did not see anything on conduct for any of these services. I thought maybe I was looking in the wrong place, but clicking around didn't find the information either. In terms of the privacy statements, [College Cooperative] really emphasizes the fact that all personally identifiable information is removed from the transcripts. I also like the idea of inviting the user to make corrections to the kept transcripts if they find an error."

"The privacy policy that most impressed me was [Public/Academic Consortium]. Their explanations were very clear and thorough, the terms well defined, and they educated the users about privacy."

"I particularly liked the one from [State Consortium], which listed each kind of information collected (e-mail zip code, IP address, etc.) with an explanation of why and how each would be used directly next to it (kind of like a table). This method went a long way to convincing me that they weren't attempting to hide anything or mislead the patron. The one I liked the least was that of [College Library Cooperative], because it wasn't very well organized, attractive, or comprehensive or detailed."

"[State Library] This was well written and easy to understand. I wonder, though, how many people actually read through such a long document."

Staff Guidelines

"[Public/Academic Consortium] This is really a very thorough handbook. I liked the emphasis on good customer service. It includes information about referrals and the confidentiality of both patron and librarian. It's interesting that the consortium has access to its own databases. I liked that when discussing user authentication and local

> resources, it said 'when in doubt, serve the client.' I also liked that they have a procedure for practice sessions and encourage staff to 'Practice often!'"
>
> "[State University] developed a Live Procedures Manual that is practically a tutorial for their specific library. The Ask A Librarian Guidelines were also very complete and great for establishing protocols. I liked their e-mail answer and VRS categories for reference questions also. The Guidelines covered academic institution situations and concerns well."
>
> "[Large Municipal Library] These guidelines were straightforward and not too involved. Their Word formatting gave them a quickly thrown together look, rather than something thought out and more formal."
>
> "[State University] The only guidelines I saw that were applicable to staff were what kinds of questions are not appropriate. Otherwise fairly sketchy on the staff side of things."
>
> "[Research Library Consortium] gave detailed instruction including logging in, what to look for on the screen, what to do if you see a certain message and how to escort the patron in the use of licensed databases. They give time limit guidelines and provide a link for other online reference guidelines. A list of databases is provided with active links to the tutorials for them. I imagine having all of this information (3 pages of small print) would be a handy guide with ready informational links for the librarian and would promote consistency of service."

The sheer volume of material available in many of the online documents made learners appreciate succinct, well-written, thoughtful policies. They admired the use of formatting techniques like bulleted lists and tables, as well as the judicious use of white space. All appreciated the wide range of policies and procedures covered, since they provide a wealth of material for use in developing or refining local library guidelines.

SHARING VIA DISCUSSION LIST

Two online discussion lists (one for each of the pair of classes offered concurrently) were supported by the Washington State Library and maintained by the project coordinator. Learners initially were instructed to subscribe themselves. However, in many cases, they were either unsuccessful or forgot. The project coordinator eventually subscribed all members of each class immediately after the orientation session. The list normally was maintained for a week to ten days after each class completed work, in case there were some final or late comments. Names were removed from each list prior to adding the new group of learners.

Many references have been made in this book to the use of these discussion lists, and the examples offered throughout this and the next chapter attest to the quality and breadth of insights that were posted. Of equal importance is the way in which this activity encouraged careful analysis of the core topics introduced in the exercises. In many cases, learners and trainers enlarged on a specific comment or extrapolated ideas from their online activities to customer service at the reference desk. Like the online meetings, the discussion list also helped develop group chemistry. Participants applauded and questioned each other's observations, recommended newfound articles, and shared anecdotes from their own libraries.

Like the transcripts of reference transactions and online meetings, the discussion list postings provide a written record of learners' thoughts from the Anytime, Anywhere Answers program. Some individuals saved these materials for future reference, adding them to the binder that was provided at orientation. For the trainers, the list offered a way to recognize and respond to astute observations, cheer individual efforts, and note progress and promote continued work, generally adding value to the discussions.

ONLINE MEETINGS

The online chat meetings represented one of the most successful and valuable of all class activities. In fact, this format subsequently was used for Statewide Virtual Reference Project committee and other meetings unrelated to the VRS training. The ability to assemble individuals geographically distant and the automatic distribution of session transcripts were great incentives for using this online format. (Not having to assign note-taking duty is a real benefit.) Some of the Anytime, Anywhere Answers classes developed extraordinary mutual understanding and respect online. One example of this is offered in the appendix F transcript.

In order to facilitate these online gatherings, the guidelines reproduced (in edited form) on the next page were used. They were discussed in the orientation session and were displayed on screen at the beginning of each meeting (see figure 3).

Figure 3. "Norms for Online Meetings"

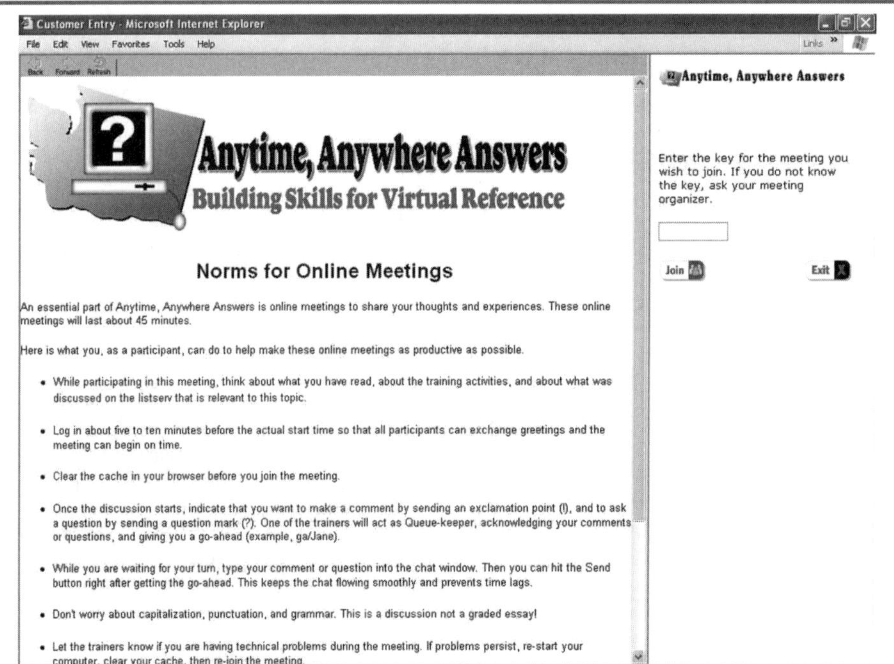

Norms for Online Meetings

An essential part of this training on Building Skills for Virtual Reference is online meetings to share your thoughts and experiences. These online meetings will focus on a variety of topics and will last about 45 minutes. You will receive the dates and times for the meetings from the trainers. Here is what you, as a participant, can do to help make these online meetings as productive as possible.

GETTTING READY

Come to the meeting prepared to participate thoughtfully. Read the required background articles and complete the activities for the week, before the meeting date. You'll be able to contribute more to the meeting as a result. Log into the website for the meeting about five to ten minutes before the actual start time so that all participants can exchange greetings and the meeting can begin on time. Clear your cache in your browser before you join the meeting. Let the trainers know in advance if you are unable to attend that week.

PARTICIPATING

Once the discussion starts, indicate that you want to make a comment by sending an exclamation point (!), and to ask a question by sending a question mark (?). One of the trainers will act as queue-keeper, acknowledging your comments or questions, and giving you a go-ahead (example, ga/Jane). While you are waiting for your turn, type your comment or question into the chat window. Then you can hit the Send button right after getting the go-ahead. This keeps the chat flowing smoothly and prevents time lags. Don't worry about capitalization, punctuation, and grammar. This is a discussion, not a graded essay!

Let the trainers know if you are having technical problems during the meeting. If problems persist, restart your computer, clear your cache, then rejoin the meeting. Don't worry if you are late for the meeting. Remember that you will receive a transcript of the meeting, including links to the PowerPoint presentation used.

STAYING ON TOPIC

Keep each posting short and to the point, addressing a single issue or thought. If the discussion strays from the topic, the trainers will refocus the meeting, referring other issues to the list for further discussion there. Be respectful of the opinions of others. Be careful with intonations of sarcasm or humor. It's easy to misinterpret meaning in a chat environment. That doesn't mean you can't make a joke, but be sure it's clear that you're joking. Enjoy this opportunity to interact in real time!

Initially, the first online chat meeting was intended to provide added chat practice using instant messaging; an open-ended topic determined by the trainers provided the focus. This approach was modified toward the end of 2003 classes due to ongoing technical problems (see chapter 9). The following weeks used virtual reference software to explore the following specific, relevant areas. For each topic, a slide show and scripted questions were incorporated to lead the discussion. Notes for trainers (not visible to learners) were also included.

Information Literacy

In the first topical meeting, each class explored the ways in which information literacy could be promoted in online reference transactions. "Information literacy" was defined as the set of skills that enable individuals to locate, evaluate, and effectively use needed information. The discussion began by recognizing that the increasing and overwhelming volume of information available—especially on the Web—will not create a better-informed society without accompanying abilities to use it efficiently. The slide show offered a brief overview of the

"Big 6 Skills" (task definition, information-seeking strategies, location and access, use of information, synthesis, and evaluation), placing them in the context of reference service.[4] Several questions were posed to guide the discussion:

> Are we missing opportunities for promoting information literacy in online real-time reference?
>
> How do you determine the approach to use in answering questions online?
>
> How can the transcripts themselves become resources for creating information literacy tools?

Participants from academic libraries were more comfortable with the concept of information literacy, noting that they tried to teach students to make decisions about choosing the best resources for their problems or assignments rather than simply providing an answer or pointing to a source. Online transactions provide new challenges, however. One learner pointed out that "we don't hear the hesitancy or wavering while the patron states what they are looking for," and "some patrons have more trouble expressing their real needs in a written environment." At the same time, the efficacy of co-browsing was cited: "they can see how to seek the information," and "When it works, it's really powerful!" All agreed on the importance of showing customers how to locate the right web page so that they can repeat the experience on their own.

Many observations were based on user experiences during Secret Patron activities:

> "I wondered why none of the libraries suggested their online article databases to answer my question."
>
> "Then the librarian just told me to look up my answer in *Consumer Reports* without considering that I was an online patron."
>
> "I know that when I'm online I feel a pressure to answer quickly, and I think that is what happened with the librarians who were helping me. Teaching skills just fell by the wayside."
>
> "During two of my visits, I felt the librarian just wanted to get rid of me. During the last, the librarian really seemed to want to help me but didn't know how to do so online. She asked me to call her and then she asked for my address so that she could mail information."

Repeated comments were made about the overuse of Google, underuse of authoritative online resources, and the need for librarians to "take charge and pace the transaction."

Over time, libraries will be able to gather a great deal of data about the questions that customers ask. One learner suggested that transcripts could be used for designing staff web pages—a kind of "virtual information rack" in which patterns or problems are identified and solutions offered.

Service Evaluation

The second online meeting asked whether evaluation and improvement are two sides of the same coin. The discussion began by recognizing that currently there are no widely accepted criteria for assessing the quality of online reference service, although studies are moving toward common definitions of success and measurement components.[5]

The discussion was guided by slides that focused on outcome measures (quality of answers), process measures (effectiveness and efficiency), economic measures (cost effectiveness), and user satisfaction. The questions posed included:

> How can the quality of answers be measured, and is this done in face-to-face reference?
>
> What are some tools that can be used to measure effectiveness and efficiency as perceived by users?
>
> How difficult is it to determine actual costs, and how can the impact on other library services be measured?
>
> Are post-transaction surveys sufficient to measure user satisfaction?
>
> How would you characterize your library's readiness for evaluation?

This meaty topic drew wide-ranging commentary in all groups. The recognition of the importance of evaluation was accompanied by the difficulty of implementing it.

> "It's easiest to measure basics like timeliness of response and accessibility, but harder to measure actual service."
>
> "Most people won't take the time to respond to open survey questions."
>
> "It seems like so many places are fitting this into already tight schedules."
>
> "The consensus seems to be that the technology will change so much so rapidly that this could all be done differently before we really get it figured out."
>
> "Remember how poor early color TV was? Maybe early VR is like that."
>
> "How do consortia determine service levels and improvement? Is it harder to implement and assess in a consortium?" [answer] "I don't think it's harder in a consortium as long as you don't get hung up on every partner being absolutely uniform."

There were many more questions asked during these discussions than there were answers, although members of every class acknowledged the potential value of transcripts as a tool for evaluating and improving service. The need to understand why virtual reference service is offered and what it is expected to accomplish was the basis for many comments. It was thought that as digital reference service was built, outcomes assessment would become more prominent. The next question one class asked was whether the outcomes originally stated remained valid as information was gathered.

Marketing

A good illustration of the ways in which the classes integrated core concepts and flowed logically from week to week is the exchange that followed the final slide in the preceding Service Evaluation meeting. The slide quoted Jo Bell Whitlatch: "Marketing and program evaluation skills will be as important as mastering the technology," which elicited this interesting exchange:

Linda:	How can a library survive if we don't promote ourselves, need to be loud and proud!
Lily:	Especially to the younger "everything is on the Internet" crowd.
Margret:	My son is in middle school and it seems that all his teachers require for research are some websites.
Lily:	Do they receive any guidelines on evaluating the info?
Margret:	Not that I am seeing. In fact, I am e-mailing one of his teachers today (14-page report with information gathered from websites only). Grrrr.

The online discussions of the Marketing Virtual Reference topic were some of the most stimulating chat meetings. An edited transcript of one such meeting is reproduced in appendix F. The slides and questions used as the meeting progressed included the following:

Does the fear of being overwhelmed by questions prevent us from actively publicizing our virtual reference services?

A marketing plan identifies the potential users of the service, outlines a strategy for attracting and keeping users, and identifies and anticipates changes to the service. Are there other things that can be achieved by it?

What data will be gathered before creating the marketing plan?

When will the plan be implemented? Is your service ready for "prime time"?

How can the impact of the marketing plan be evaluated? How can we know what worked and what didn't?

By the time this final online meeting took place for each class, there was little doubt in anyone's mind about the direct link between marketing and service usage. Those libraries with high usage were those that implemented thoughtfully designed web pages, integrated their promotional efforts with service delivery, and evaluated the results.

SUMMARY

The cumulated experience of class activities was extraordinary for everyone involved in the Anytime, Anywhere Answers program. Trainers who were not scheduled for the next round of training talked about withdrawal symptoms and volunteered eagerly to work with another class of learners. The curriculum developers marveled at the treasure trove of information produced by the learners. The project director repeatedly told colleagues that it was the "most exciting experience of my career." When asked to complete the follow-up skills assessment three months after finishing the training program, learners added numerous compliments and thanks for the opportunity to participate. We look forward eagerly to the next year of classes!

As has been stated previously, virtual reference is one facet of the larger world of reference service. Nothing affects the quality of the service more than the behaviors of the library staff who provide it. In the next chapter, we will examine aspects of model reference behaviors as they are used in the online environment. We draw heavily on the Anytime, Anywhere Answers learners' reports on their Secret Patron activities to illustrate the many ways in which librarians succeed and fail in providing responsive, appropriate answers to customer queries.

NOTES

1. The Walking Billboards exercise was taken from Edward E. Scannell (contributor) and John W. Newstrom, *Still More Games Trainers Play* (New York: McGraw-Hill, 1991).
2. Steve Coffman and Abe Anhang, "The Great Reference Debate," *American Libraries* 33, no. 3 (March 2002): 50+.
3. Patricia L. Owens, "Focus Group Results: March 2002," prepared for the Washington State Library, Statewide Virtual Reference Project, http://www.statelib.wa.gov/libraries/projects/virtualRef/activities/.
4. See Michael B. Eisenberg and Robert E. Berkowitz, *Information Problem-Solving: The Big6 Skills Approach to Library and Information Skills Instruction* (Stamford, Conn.: Ablex, 1990).
5. An extensive examination of quality measures is available in Charles R. McClure et al., *Statistics, Measures and Quality Standards for Assessing Digital Reference Library Services: Guidelines and Procedures* (Syracuse, N.Y.: Information Resources, 2002).

8 Model Reference: Online Behaviors

The most difficult aspect of digital reference service involves incorporating model reference interview techniques into an online transaction. This chapter offers observations on incorporating guidelines such as RUSA's "Guidelines for Behavioral Performance of Reference and Information Services Professionals" (see bibliography) for setting the tone, getting the question straight, keeping the customer informed, providing information, and follow-up. These considerations were mentioned briefly as part of the discussion of core competencies in chapter 3.

Like in-person and telephone reference communications, the online interaction between the librarian and customer is complex. A satisfactory transaction may be the simple transfer of brief data to answer a quick information question. ("What year did the Detroit Tigers last win the World Series?") However, it is equally likely that an interchange of questions and clarifications can lead to a lengthy search strategy, guidance in the evaluation of resources, or the provision of extensive information. ("Who has refuted that William Shakespeare authored the works attributed to him, and why?") The positive or negative behavior of the virtual reference operator can dramatically influence the customer's perception of success. Almost every reference librarian has experienced a situation in which he or she spent a great deal of time working with a customer without producing the wanted information, yet still received a profuse expression of gratitude for the attention and effort. This can happen online as well as at the desk.

A significant factor for the VRS training classes was the diversity of libraries represented by the participants. The goal of the academic library is to support study and research, leading to a focus on instruction and guidance in research. Library media centers in K–12 schools are even more centered on teaching students how to locate and choose information. Staff members in public libraries concentrate on satisfying the customers' demands for answers, but their work is complicated by the need to serve students whose instructors frown on providing solutions rather than instruction. In a consortium where virtual reference serves these differing communities and is staffed by representatives from multitype libraries, providers must be able to offer flexible approaches based on customer needs. By observing the behaviors of their counterparts at other institutions around the country, the VRS training participants were exposed to a variety of welcoming phrases, interview techniques, script use, search strategies, citation methods, follow-up suggestions, and more. Both effective and failed transactions offered useful information that could be incorporated into their own work on the job.

Participants in the VRS training were not given a formula for using model reference behaviors in the same way the trainees in previous Effective Reference Performance training had been. Because the training focused on constructivist learning, participants were encouraged to choose from among alternate methods based on the Secret Patron and other class experiences. The learner's personal style combined with his or her local library collections, policies, and customer preferences influenced those choices. The curriculum and training materials did include the latest approaches, resources, and debate on virtual reference service. Learners were required to read the RUSA guidelines and apply them to the Secret Patron activity, in which they used service from several libraries. The curriculum developers and trainers recognized that the RUSA guidelines need some adaptation for remote service delivery. Learners were asked to decide whether they received good service based on specific criteria that incorporate model reference behaviors and are part of the evaluation checklist used for the Secret Patron sessions. (See figure 4.)

Figure 4. Online Secret Patron Scenario

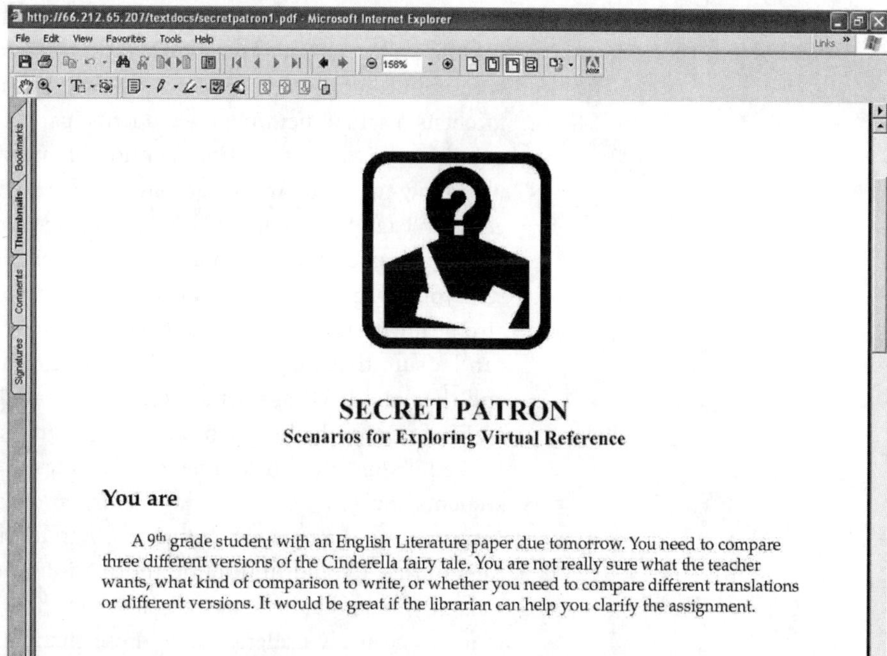

SETTING THE TONE

One learner observed, "Remember that the patron cannot see you!" Keeping in touch even with canned phrases seems very polite. Since 80 percent of communication is nonverbal and we're depending totally on a very strange verbal form of communication, a lot is getting left out and it's easy to be misinterpreted. While there is no way to provide direct eye contact or offer a friendly voice in a text-based chat reference session, there are other ways to communicate welcome.

The manner in which a library chooses to implement its service helps shape the tenor of the library operator's initial greeting. VRS training participants overwhelmingly preferred the use of a "real" name (whether fictitious or the actual name of the operator) rather than a generic one (e.g., Librarian18). A personal, informal greeting with the use of the customer's name was also well received, such as "Hi, Bob. How can I help you today?" In most cases, the librarian revealed personal interest in the query and readiness to help by the phrases he or she used to respond to the customer. Scripted messages that seemed to substitute for real clarification or a personal reply were perceived as poor service, while the thoughtful integration and individualization of them was recognized as efficient. Here are relevant observations from one Secret Patron report:

> "I visited [Metropolitan Public Library]. My scenario is a middle-school teacher seeking sources of info for her students studying world religions, specifically Judaism. I was to ask about the difference between kosher and non-kosher kitchens, who monitors them, and how to be sure one is really kosher. The link was a little difficult to find—if I hadn't been working on this, I would not have known to go to 'Reference Services' and then look for something about talking to a librarian. The text and logos were VERY small.
>
> I logged on and quickly got the canned response of 'A librarian will be with you in about a minute.' About a minute later I received a generic 'What is your question?' message. After 2–3 more minutes with no further interaction, I was asked if I meant home or restaurant kitchens. I said either one, my students just wanted to learn about the definitions. This was my first mention of 'my students,' but there was no follow-up as to what age, etc. The next message sent was the generic 'Page Sent,' followed by a message from the librarian, who never addressed me by name or introduced him/herself, saying 'I've sent you a page that should answer your question.' I asked if it would also deal with the issue of who checks on these kitchens and how one can be sure that they are really kosher. Another long wait followed, and then another 'Page sent' message appeared. The page popped up and once again the librarian said 'This should answer your question.' I asked if s/he could recommend more sites or starting points for my students for self-study and eventually another 'page sent' message appeared and the response from the librarian that this should be helpful and that I could find more information at my local library. I said 'Thank you' and ended the call, at which time I got a pop-up survey that was basically useless (grade these elements from 1–5, but all the questions seemed the same) and a list of three websites as links, which was a nice touch had I wanted to revisit and bookmark them.

I felt that the librarian was totally disengaged—no reference interview, no probing for sources I had checked or what kinds of sources I wanted—just pushed the web pages and left. I surmise they have pages bookmarked and sorted and push them routinely in response to questions in given subject areas. I felt much of the script was canned, especially the 'local library' statement.

I'm sure there are time elements involved and issues about serving local patrons first, but if canned scripts are going to be used, they might be structured around reference interview questions, such as 'What kind of sources would be helpful?' and 'What level of information are you seeking?' I didn't feel that there was time for me to review the sources and determine whether they were helpful and that question was never asked. Whether this was because I was not local and their policy is to short-shrift out-of-towners or because the librarian had a quota or other time constraint, I can't say. I was not invited back, obviously, as in 'If these sources don't answer your questions, please contact us again.' I got the sense that this was a chore, something to dispatch as quickly and efficiently as possible, but I did not feel particularly welcome.

I would suggest that they review how committed they are to this service—if they are overwhelmed, reduce it to local patrons only or drop it altogether. I think Joe Janes is right in his 'too much, too soon' analysis of VR, when it means that the product is second rate. It does more harm than good to throw something up without the necessary support or training or commitment."

Compare that experience with this one:

"In my secret patron assignment, I pretended to be a high school student who was working on an extra credit assignment. I was instructed to misspell a few words and not use correct punctuation. My question was: who were the pepins and what was their dynasty?

[Municipal Public Library] is part of the [Consortium], which uses LSSI software. When I connected, it indicated that the librarian's name was Connie, at [College Library]. She was fast and efficient, sending me a page right off the bat, after a canned greeting (Hello Bill, welcome to your [Consortium] reference session. I'm looking at your question right now; it will be a minute.). Connie obviously understood my question from the get-go, and she pushed a page to me within a couple of minutes. Then she clarified a bit (Do you mean Pepin and the Charlemagne era?) and then sent me another page. Both pages were helpful and authoritative, but I didn't feel like there was a human on the other side, just a robot pushing pages.

[County Public Library] also uses LSSI and they are not part of a consortium. My librarian's name was Ms. Green, and she was also fast and efficient, pushing me a couple of good websites. She asked if these pages answered my question, and asked if I had any other questions. Again, the librarian was knowledgeable, helpful and efficient, but not very personable.

Overall, I thought the service I received was good. . . . The librarians who knew my topic, and didn't have any trouble locating relevant

> websites were very efficient, but I didn't really feel like I had interacted with a human being. When I'm answering virtual reference questions, I will try to incorporate a little more human interaction in the session, so that the patron knows that they are talking to a person, not a search engine."

These reports are typical and point to the importance of Anytime, Anywhere Answers activities in helping library staff members to understand what it feels like at the customer end of the Web. Learners readily empathized with impersonal and curt treatment, and they were determined to better themselves.

GETTING THE QUESTION STRAIGHT

Reference service guidelines, as well as graduate school and other instruction on effective information interviews, emphasize the need for clarifying questions through the use of open-ended probes, the use of paraphrase, and other techniques. When reference librarians gather, they love to tell stories about "how I figured out what Mrs. Smith *really* wanted" and the illogical—to them—ways that customers seek information. Taking every query at face value leads to misinterpretation, frustration, wrong assumptions, and unsatisfactory service.

VRS training participants reported this part of the online reference interview as the one most prone to failure. It is hard to determine the cause of this—the perception that online answers must be delivered as quickly as possible, the lack of visual and oral cues, an overreliance on Google, competing work duties (handling multiple online customers, combining desk or phone service with online, reading reviews), the assumption that a typed question is well reasoned, inadequate training, or other problems. The fact remains that many queries were treated superficially. Rarely were encouraging questions asked, such as "Please tell me more about your topic," "Can you give me additional information?" and "How much information do you need?" When virtual reference operators did offer a thoughtful, thorough interview, learners expressed admiration and reported skills that could be emulated. Here are some examples from Secret Patron assignments:

> "I went to [Public Library]. . . . There was no greeting. I signed on and typed in my question (a listing of plays in Chicago in July) and received an abrupt 'What week in July?' A question she didn't need the answer to, in the end. Then I sat wondering what was happening (the long silence). I finally was pushed a page. Before I could look at it I was pushed a second page and told to let them know if there was anything else, goodbye. All very abrupt and annoying."

> "My scenario was fairly simple yet I thought it represented the real world. My question was 'What is the average temperature of Brazil?' when what I really wanted was information about Rio in September during my 'trip.' Patrons often ask a question which isn't what they really need at all. As I am sure we all know.
>
> [University Library], the only academic, was the biggest disappointment. After a wait, he said my question would take more time and could I give him my e-mail? End of session. I did receive an e-mail

> with 'climate info' pasted into the message with the website included, but there was no follow-up with the patron at all.
>
> [County Public Library] and [different County Public Library] had similar characteristics. Both of them had some technical difficulties and while they were busy, I slipped my 'real' query into the mix and neither of them noticed. They were caught on the fact of average temperature and did not follow up when I actually mentioned my real need. [The first library] asked if I had enough but did not notice when I said 'wondered about things in rio in sept' and [the second library] was bogged down in tech problems so when I was real clear with my question, she missed it completely.
>
> All of these libraries asked for my question before we connected. This seems good on the surface because they can start 'answering' the question but this way makes it easy to miss conducting any reference interview. The public libraries seemed to have a more developed system to connect more personally to patrons and I like the fact that they both told me what to expect. Posing as a 'non-pushy' patron, I accepted the responses I was given since I did tell them what I really wanted and was ignored and would feel that 'the librarian really didn't help me much.' This was a useful educational exercise and I have learned . . . a lot."

As shown by this report, technical difficulties are very distracting. Good listening skills (or in this case, careful reading) are necessary. Here is another, more positive report:

> "My scenario was a 65-year-old woman asking the medical term for heel spurs. Further information if needed was that my doctor wasn't very sympathetic and my orthotics weren't helping.
>
> [County Public Library] . . . overall left the best impression because of the excellent interaction with the librarian despite some technical difficulties. [She] was excellent and sympathetic. It was really like speaking to a skilled reference librarian. It was the only site that listed the librarian by name (Ms. G . . . whether true or not I don't know, but it made a good impression). She was the only one who initially clarified the question. The dialogue was excellent, incorporated all of the elements we have been talking about. The initial script while telling you to wait noted 'Please feel free to browse the links found on the library's website to the left.' She worked through the database page problems with aplomb, asking, 'Did you receive the article?' And later 'Please tell me if you got it.'
>
> I want to remember the importance of good scripts and dialogue with the user. After receiving good information this makes a big difference in the overall impression of the service."

These reports illustrate the importance of the interplay between good reference interview techniques and well-written, appropriately used scripted messages. Continued interactivity between the librarian and customer is critical to ensuring satisfaction. The reports also point out potential problems caused by services which request that the customer enter the question as part of the initial log-on process. Like most procedures, there are both positive and negative aspects that must be taken into account. Good training helps mitigate the possibility that question clarification will be bypassed.

KEEPING THE CUSTOMER INFORMED

The lack of physical clues for either librarian or customer can create awkward situations, especially when technology balks. A missing encyclopedia volume is a visible and obvious sign of difficulty, while slow communication—whether caused by hardware or software at either end of the transaction—is not. Keeping a steady flow of information about what the service provider is doing is easy compared to dealing with the gremlins that inhabit the Web. The ease is relative, however. VRS training emphasized that in providing continuing feedback to the customer, the librarian should:

- Ask whether the customer wanted to see how to find the answer.
- Offer responses that are clear, easy to read, and free of library jargon or personal opinion.
- Keep the customer informed about progress in finding an answer, providing a time estimate when needed.
- Let the customer know what is being done, e.g., still looking, pushing a web page, escorting, etc.
- Provide help with and information about any technical difficulties.

It is worthwhile to imagine some of the techniques used effectively at the reference desk and imagine them in the online environment. Virtual reference lends itself well to some methods that are less obvious at the desk. For example, a librarian working at the reference desk doesn't always remember to turn her monitor toward the customer to explain what she is finding in the catalog or a database. But by pushing web pages or co-browsing during a virtual reference transaction, she is displaying information directly to the customer. On the other hand, in the physical library, a librarian can observe when the customer is confused by the use of library jargon, and can translate terms such as "stacks" and "Interlibrary Loan" with a smile. Online, the lack of clarity can cause customer disappearance.

When a difficult search for needed information leads reference staff on a prolonged tour of resources in the library, the customer can see the procedures being used and perhaps can sympathize with the complexity of his or her request. Without continuing explanation and sharing of progress, the online customer may assume lack of expertise, telecommunications failure, or abandonment. By the time the librarian remembers to say, "This is going to take more time. Could I contact you by e-mail or phone when I locate the information?" the customer may have resorted to Yahoo.

For the library staff member working at the reference desk, helping the patron with such technical matters as the use of the card catalog, the photocopier, or the microfilm reader is all part of the day's work. Learning how to aid a patron who is encountering proxy server problems or is being repeatedly dropped from a session comes less naturally. While Anytime, Anywhere

Answers could not directly provide instruction in difficulties that result from local configurations and applications, the program did offer learners a valuable opportunity to see the effects from a customer's viewpoint. The ability to successfully guide customers through technical trouble requires local training and continued practice, as well as good documentation and support.

Here is an example of a Secret Patron report that illustrates "keeping the customer informed":

> "My initial question was 'Do you know of any good websites on Galileo?' What I really wanted was the wording of Pope John Paul's pardon of Galileo.
>
> [Regional Public Library] never picked up my call, or at least it didn't look like they did. I sent a couple of 'hello?' messages and after 8 minutes of no answer, no clue, I hung up. The transcript I received did actually have messages from '[Consortium] Librarian A' stating they had just experienced technical problems. They asked 'are you trying to find websites on Galileo?' and then proceeded to send me pages. This was followed by 'you can take a look at these' and 'are you still there?' It was only then that I realized I was no longer connected and suggested I contact them again if I needed further assistance. I thought it was odd that they would go through all of that searching and sending without having a response to their initial question to me.
>
> [County Public Library] answered very quickly, didn't do a reference interview, and proceeded to send me pages. The pages were not showing up on my screen. When I asked about that I was told the URLs would show up in my transcript. I eked out additional information on what I was looking for while the pages were being sent along, not because I was being asked for additional information but because I was feeling all awash in the site-pushing and I couldn't tell if what they were sending would answer my question. The librarian then saw I was asking a more specific question and the search changed. As the chat went on I could actually start to see the pages being found. The librarian wrote short messages saying something about the pages being sent but I wondered how to use the sites, not readily seeing what I was looking for. The librarian was good at this point to let me know that she/he was still looking and that the actual text of the pardon was a bit tricky to find. Perhaps the sites were being sent just to keep me busy while the real website was being scouted out. We ended up with one site that looked promising and a suggestion to e-mail someone at catholic.org with my question. This librarian was the most personable, even though nameless. They seemed to be the most at ease and the short descriptions sent with the URLs were a nice touch. This was also the only site that didn't have technical problems during the session. A list of the URLs visited showed up on the browser after I exited the chat and the transcript arrived about 3 hours later.
>
> I snuck into [Metropolitan Public Library] by using a fake zip code. Again, no reference interview and plenty o' sites pushed. One site was just an Infotrac search page, with no terms entered. This was followed by the message 'click on each article for more information.'

> A couple of times a gray box appeared with a confusing message about present site and new site. It was unclear to me what to do and I actually lost a site that looked promising to me. I notified the librarian about it, asking to have the site sent again. This was followed by an apology saying they were having technical difficulties. Some more sites were sent and another message 'sorry I keep getting booted.' I said I could call back and asked if there was a better time for chat. 'Not really' was the answer. I then asked if the information could be e-mailed to me. 'Librarian4' said that would be fine and something would be sent as soon as it was found. I received a transcipt and a separate e-mail with information on the document I was looking for. The e-mail was signed with a real name.
>
> It may be that since I was asking for websites, I was pushed such an abundance of them. The thing that surprised me though was the lack of in-between comments or questions like 'does this look like the sort of thing you want?' It seemed to be very geared into the machinery rather than conversation or communication. I think starting out with a conversation, a reference interview done without hurling URLs around would have been a much more pleasant exchange for me."

The preceding report illustrates many ways in which interactive continuing communication is needed in the online environment and also what happens when it is missing.

PROVIDING INFORMATION

"Satisfycing" (a blend of "satisfying" and "sufficing") and "good enough" are terms frequently used by virtual reference experts when discussing customer expectations of information provided in answer to questions. One learner was troubled by the frequent use of Google and similar sources by virtual reference providers:

> "I would hate to think that we are beginning to mimic our patrons in trusting a more convenient source, knowing it probably isn't the best, rather than taking a little more time to find higher quality information."

As information professionals, virtual reference operators are very concerned that customers receive authoritative, up-to-date, appropriate responses to queries. Maintaining a high standard for service is seen as a qualitative factor that differentiates libraries from commercial fee-based services and generic search engines. VRS training offered these guidelines:

- Provide authoritative information appropriate to the need and interest of the customer.
- Offer sufficient time to determine whether the information found answers the question to the customer's satisfaction. Don't rush them by pushing too much information.
- Cite the source of the information.
- Ask whether more sources are wanted.

- Recognize when questions need to be referred elsewhere or can be more effectively answered through e-mail.

In terms of VRS learner experiences, there was a very mixed bag of behaviors that succeeded or failed to ensure that customers received the most reliable information. In most cases, the information provided was relevant, although often it was incomplete or confusing. There were many cases of overkill, when learners were bombarded with unexplained URLs. Transactions frequently were rushed, and citations often were not included. Rarely did the virtual reference provider ask whether more or different information was needed, and referrals were almost nonexistent. (This latter may be a symptom of "GLS"—Greedy Librarian Syndrome, or a reluctance to give up a question or admit that local resources are insufficient.) When a session was difficult, either because of the complexity of the question or technical problems, the "secret patron" appreciated when the virtual reference operator offered to provide information in a subsequent e-mail message. However, that was not the norm. Some operators apparently assumed that the transcript sent to the customer would be sufficient. Furthermore, not all software provides transcripts, either automatically or on request.

Many of the previously quoted reports offer examples related to the quality of information provided. Here are two more:

> "[F]irst they didn't clarify the question and answered the wrong one (gave me information on Tommy Dorsey instead of Thomas A. Dorsey) but the interaction was very good and the librarian was very gracious when he/she realized the mistake. As a contrast, [Metropolitan Public Library] actually gave me 'correct' information, but the librarian pushed too many pages one after another without any explanation."

> "I was to ask about credit cards that earn frequent flyer miles. . . . [Municipal Public Library] fed me a few sites but didn't respond effectively to the feedback I provided, but the sites were very flashy and commercial—they didn't have the look of someplace that I would trust for unbiased financial information. On the other hand, I was impressed that this was the only service that recommended a book. . . . On the downside of this, they fed me a citation for it from Amazon, and didn't offer to see if the library owned the book or could borrow it for me. I found this odd, since it seems like part of the benefit of a chat service would be to promote the library's other resources."

Working with a customer in an online reference transaction offers wonderful opportunities for information literacy instruction. Here are excerpts from an online class chat meeting:

Learner A: I know some of our librarians feel pressure when they are doing VR at the ref desk.

Learner B: Makes me curious if that's really the patron's expectation or only ours—that it has to be fast if it's VR.

Learner C: It is a totally different feeling when the computer chimes as opposed to the phone ringing or a patron stopping at the desk.

Trainer A: I would feel under pressure at the desk to 'finish up' online quickly, in case a 'real' patron came in.

Learner A: It doesn't matter whose misperception . . . we need to take charge and pace the transaction . . . and if they bail, they bail.

Trainer A: Do you simply push a web page with the answer? Show the patron how to do a search? Suggest other sources?

Learner A: I think the response depends on the question, to some degree (fast fact vs. research type question).

Trainer A: You almost need to know what kind of connection the patron has, whether they can used restricted databases, and how much time they have, in addition to the reference interview.

Learner A: Perhaps what is needed are more "ready reference" pages with links for the librarian to use?

Trainer B: Yes, you can often tell if the person wants to learn some thing for a future problem or just get the answer now.

Trainer A: And the patron could be shown how to navigate those pages.

Learner B: That's more in line with information literacy, pushing more than generic search engines.

The preceding discussion touches on the complex nature of online reference work and the competing demands of time, resources, and customer need. It was frequently observed in all of the classes that continued practice provides greater comfort with web-based tools and resources, as well as experience in handling a variety of questions and customer situations.

FOLLOW-UP

Like a good golf swing, the ability to follow through a virtual reference transaction has a great effect on success. VRS training suggested that at the close of a session, librarians should:

Ask whether the information found was a satisfactory answer to the question.

Ask whether the customer had any other questions.

Encourage the customer to use the service again.

Thank the customer.

Ask the customer to evaluate the experience with the service. (This may take the form of an online survey.)

In the best Secret Patron experiences, most or all of the aforementioned behaviors took place. In most cases, however, at least some of the steps were ignored. Here is an example of mixed follow-up:

> "I was able to ask my first question and she gave me a good answer and listed her reference book as a source. Before I could ask my additional questions, she asked if she could e-mail the other answers to me

because she had people waiting at the reference desk who needed help. She did e-mail later but didn't ask if these answered my question. She only thanked me for using their service. The sources she did give me were good and answered my questions, though."

Some transactions ended badly:

> "My assignment was to be a parent who is looking for information on the safety of a 1997 Chevy Malibu, as I am considering purchasing this for my teenage daughter. I also want to know about laws restricting teenage driving.
>
> [County Public Library] was the worst experience as far as getting an answer. This librarian told me that I would find the information in the April issue of *Consumer Reports*. I asked if they would have info on crash tests and safety recalls and said I thought *Consumer Reports* was for new cars. Next message from her said that I should try *Road and Track* or *Car and Driver.* So then I asked if there was information online. I mean, hello, I am asking online. She didn't ask whether I had access to article databases or suggest using them. . . . I had been noticing that the librarian's name appeared as though she was in a state other than that of the library I had logged on. So, when I asked for the information about driving laws in 'my' state, I mentioned that it looked like she was somewhere else. Her response was that she was running two sessions at once and that I should check with a source for my state for law information. . . . I stated that I went to my library and didn't know how I got to her. At that point the librarian ended the session. The message indicated that she ended it rather than us getting bumped off."

There were a number of positive reports. One learner noted that a city public library transcript added, "Please use our service often." A public university transcript ended with an e-mail address and a request for further questions or feedback. One public library operator that had been less than effective during the interaction did follow quickly with an e-mail that "listed a number of books that the library owned, as well as a summary and table of contents from one of the books that was right on topic."

Learners encountered a variety of online surveys at the end of transactions. Some appeared to be specific to a library, while software vendors apparently designed others. While there is much of interest in these evaluation instruments, judging them went beyond the scope of the VRS training.

SUMMARY

Trainers made a number of observations on the Secret Patron assignments that summarize the results of learner experience. A number of common themes ran through all eight classes.

> "Well, it looks like the secret patron activity was interesting and a great learning experience! Not only is it kind of fun to be on the 'other side' (the patron side) but when you know it isn't just your coworker down the hall, or in your consortium for that matter, it makes the

> experience all the more interesting. One question that came to our mind was 'Do librarians have higher standards?'
>
> A lot of the comments you all submitted seemed to stress the impersonal-ness of the scripted messages and that pages were being pushed too quickly and without warning. This is really something we all need to work on: making the transactions online as personable as we would at the reference desk with our 'solid' patrons. One learner noted it was nice to get the URL before it was pushed, and that is a pretty easy way to give a heads-up and provide some context for why you are sending that URL. Other comments on the lack of a 'reference interview' process resonate with what all of you noted in one way or another.
>
> Another interesting comment about using a 'real name' vs. something like SLS Librarian: this might be something we all might want to reconsider for our services. We are sometimes so hung up on all of the privacy issues (patron and librarian) that the whole process may just become overly impersonal.
>
> The reference interview process, a professional but conversational tone, and keeping the user informed of what is going on/going to happen came up again and again. In both the digital and the analog worlds, the 'personal touch' seems really to be crucial, doesn't it!
>
> Our Secret Patron (or, as one of you discovered on one occasion, not-so-secret-patron) assignments gave everyone a chance to be on the other side with people who were totally not connected with them in any way—much in the same way our patrons see us. So, I think it left everyone with a lot to think about in terms of customer service and service quality, and the entire digital reference process."

Finally, here is a learner's summary reaction to Secret Patron exercises:

> "I was greeted personally, made to feel welcome, and had my question clarified with both open and closed questions. Responses were clear and easy to follow and the librarian kept me informed about progress and what she was doing. Pushed a great web page. . . . Nice finish—asked if my question was answered and if I had other questions, thanked me and encouraged me to use the service again. I was really pleased with the transaction and this was supported by the transcript."

This final comment underscores one of the most useful aspects of digital reference in relation to the larger world of library information services. In addition to the careful analysis of transaction transcripts, the correlation of transcripts with online survey responses provides the possibility of comparing user satisfaction with the actual interaction between the library operator and the customer. While it is not always possible to determine the exact nature of understanding or miscommunication in a reference transaction, some conclusions can be made. For example, when the survey question "Did you receive the answer you were looking for?" is checked "No," a review of the related transcript may reveal several possibilities. The librarian may have stated "I'm sorry, but the library does not subscribe to that journal," with an offer to request the material from another source which was refused by the customer. Alternatively, the customer might misspell a name (of a person, disease, place, etc.) with the result that the librarian could not locate information. (To quote one learner report, "Typos seem part of this form of reference.") There is also the possibility that erroneous information was provided—and there are also questions for which there is no answer, such as "Could you provide a copy of a Mayan Codex that's been missing for 500 years?"

By exposing learners to a range of services at diverse libraries, delivered by unknown library staff members, the Secret Patron activity revealed to learners the great variety of reference behaviors, model and otherwise. The result was a group of thoughtful participants. They returned to their libraries with enthusiasm and eagerness to implement what they had learned.

No training is complete until it is evaluated. Our VRS training used a number of tools and methods to determine the effectiveness of the classes—their content, activities, and instructors. We also reviewed materials and online applications to ensure that what we used was as up-to-date and easy to use as possible. In the final chapter, we will look at both the ways we assessed our work and what our learners told us about it. In one case, learners from an academic library used their training experience to present a day-long training workshop to their own colleagues. There is no happier example of the way in which Anytime, Anywhere Answers resulted in continuing education.

9 Evaluation, Modification, and Follow-up

Because many aspects of digital reference service are evolving rapidly, it is important to assess training from both trainers' and learners' perspectives and modify subsequent offerings in response to current needs. In addition, it is important to revisit the evaluation process after the training has been in use for a period of time. The VRS project used a variety of tools, including evaluation forms, trainer debriefings, and consultation with interested parties, such as Steering Committee members and colleagues. The online reports from learners and the chat meeting transcripts were also beneficial in determining which aspects of the training were more or less effective than others. No one was modest in offering their opinions.

EVALUATION FORMS

Appendix A provides copies of the various assessment tools used throughout the Anytime, Anywhere Answers program. Those that were used by learners for self-assessment of core competencies (Internet reference skills and Windows multitasking abilities) were discussed in chapter 3. In order to determine the effectiveness of the training itself, three different forms were used at various points. During the in-person orientation, the "Initial Skills Assessment" was given to learners following a discussion of the core competencies needed in order to provide high-quality virtual reference service. Using a range from one ("not confident") to seven ("completely confident"), learners were asked to indicate their judgment of their personal skill level in a number of abilities related to both general and virtual reference. These included:

- chat reference communication and use of scripts
- reference interview
- Internet and database searching
- critical thinking, including finding, using, and evaluating information on the Internet

- collaborative browsing
- evaluating reference transcripts
- using Windows
- technical troubleshooting
- applying reference policies online
- improving and upgrading knowledge and skills

The project coordinator collected and tallied the forms for comparison among different classes and also to provide a baseline measurement for a follow-up assessment that learners filled out three months after the completion of each class. Overall, these initial assessments offered similar patterns. Relatively few answers fell in either the one ("not confident") or seven ("completely confident") range, and most settled comfortably in the three to five mid-level of confidence. While some individuals scored themselves higher or lower than their classmates, this appeared to be at least partly a function of their familiarity or experience with online reference service.

At the end of the final week of each class, participants were asked to complete an "Evaluation of Training" form and submit it to the project coordinator by e-mail, fax, or mail. The evaluation form addressed training goals and learner objectives and also asked for written comments. Using a rating scale of five (high) to zero (low), questions covered curriculum content, activities and assignments, the value of exploration and discovery, trainer support, and overall impressions. Learner objectives included the ability to identify current resources, conduct an effective chat reference interview, identify needed virtual reference policies and procedures, use chat transcripts for improvement, and introduce information literacy skills to online patrons. They also were asked what aspects of the training were most beneficial, and which needed improvement. Finally, we requested their general observations.

While all learners completed the "Initial Skills Assessment" in class, it is not surprising that a lesser number submitted evaluation forms. Approximately one-third of those who completed the entire training course returned evaluations. The results were highly gratifying. Sixty percent of respondents gave an overall rating of five—the highest mark—for the training goals. The other 40 percent checked four. There were no lower ratings in this category. Learner objectives were also highly scored (most at five or four). The sprinkling of lower numbers indicated that some attention might be needed in the area of information literacy instruction. A handful of learners rated their ability to conduct an effective reference interview at three. Some class participants requested the inclusion of hands-on chat practice, especially for those learners whose libraries did not currently offer the service.

The most frequently cited beneficial portion of the training was visiting and using current virtual reference services. The Secret Patron exercises were singled out for high praise, although one learner "thought it somewhat unethical to pretend to be a patron and use another librarian's time and skills for training purposes."

> "I loved doing the secret patron thing. I learned a lot from that."
>
> "It was *very* useful to visit other libraries and compare the chat services."

> "Exercises—especially secret patron and reviewing transcripts, and then thinking about and reporting back to the group."

> "It was interesting visiting all the other library websites to see what other institutions are doing. Hopefully, we can learn from other people's mistakes and not make as many of our own."

> "The 'secret patron' assignment really helped me understand what a patron values (knowing the librarian's name was very important to me and now I'll be sure to introduce myself to all VR patrons). The trainers were excellent and made the experience a positive one."

A number of suggestions for improvement were made. Among the suggestions were more instruction in conducting a reference interview, reducing the number of required readings, and solving the technical problems associated with online chat meetings. A couple of learners felt that five weeks was too long—or too short.

> "More hands-on; i.e., more practice with using VR, either in a simulated service with the instructors or more visits to current services, though that doesn't allow us to test our skills as the providers of the service."

> "Technology! Tried to attend one meeting from home and was completely unsuccessful. Also had problems viewing slides at every other online meeting. This is probably not an issue directly in anyone's control."

> "We had the opportunity to practice as a secret patron asking questions, but practice answering questions (maybe as a secret librarian), sending URLs, and pushing pages would also be very beneficial."

> "Time frame—5 weeks was very short—not enough time to do assignments and readings."

Three months after the end of each class, a "Follow-up Skills Assessment" form was sent to class participants. (After the first six classes, the project coordinator converted it to an electronic form to make it easier for learners to complete and return it as an e-mail attachment.) Again, the return rate was one-third. This form was identical to the "Initial Skills Assessment," but also included a second section in which learners reported their actual use of skills they had acquired through the training. In the identical portion of the form, confidence levels were reported as higher than they had been on orientation day. Since many of the participants began active work as chat reference providers after the training, this can explain some of the improvement. It is also worth noting that participants repeatedly saw the broader applications of the training to general reference work—the use of the skills in any aspect of daily work undoubtedly reinforced the training. In the new section of the form, they were asked if they were using the skills they had learned on the job, and if so, to estimate what percentage of them they used. Four categories were offered, ranging from a low of 10–25 percent to a high of 100 percent. Only one person indicated the lowest percentage, while three reported using 100 percent of learned skills. Twenty-nine percent estimated 25–50 percent use and 43 percent reported 50–75 percent use. These results underline the participants' perception of the continuing usefulness of the training.

A second question asked whether they had any indication from customers that their approach to virtual reference service had improved as a result of training, and if so to specify how. The answers were evenly split. Of those who answered "yes," communicating effectively throughout a transaction and ensuring that customers received the needed information were most frequently cited. The final question asked whether their supervisors or colleagues had indicated that the library benefited from the learner's participation in the training. Two-thirds answered "yes," most often noting "skills shared with colleagues" as a plus. They also cited greater customer satisfaction, improved procedures or policies, and improved web page interfaces. While few added other comments, a couple are noteworthy:

> "We did not have a chat reference service in place before the beginning of training so it is difficult to gauge how much we have improved."
>
> "The only drawback for me is that I don't spend enough time working virtual reference (and no spare time to practice) to retain all of the valuable skills I learned in the training. Often, I remember that I knew how to do something but can't now."

More than sixty library staff members from seventeen libraries participated in the Anytime, Anywhere Answers classes. Several reference managers attended the orientation session but did not continue with the online activities. Certificates of completion were awarded to 90 percent of those who participated beyond the orientation day, which speaks to the quality of the training and its ability to hold the interest of learners over several weeks of remote work.

TRAINER DEBRIEFINGS

Immediately following the completion of the first two classes in December 2002, a one-hour conference call was scheduled for the trainers, curriculum developers, and the project coordinator. One much-discussed issue was the discomfort one learner had expressed about the Secret Patron activity. Context for the exercise was offered, and it was suggested that more time during orientation should be devoted to discussing its rationale and value. One trainer had developed and shared a series of "cheat sheets" that outlined orientation day activities and offered both essential information and tips. It was suggested that these be incorporated into the trainer web page. Several trainers were frustrated by the time needed to set up identity-neutral e-mail accounts and to practice using instant messaging during orientation. It was agreed that more experience would either resolve the problems or identify alternatives. The scheduling of classes over the Thanksgiving holiday was noted as a real-time constraint. The next classes (which began shortly after this debriefing) were also scheduled over a holiday period, and the recommendation to provide an additional week or so for learners to complete assignments was implemented. A significant part of the call was devoted to appreciation and enthusiasm on the part of the trainers. All felt that the curriculum offered both balance and breadth, and were delighted by the participation of learners. It was recognized that the experience was still very new, and that more tweaking would be necessary to make the curriculum as responsive as possible to learners' needs and wants.

There were groupings of trainers at three institutions—the University of Washington, Washington State University, and Seattle Public Library—which encouraged ongoing discussion about the training classes. Current classes were compared with previous ones, assignments were shared, and advice given. This led to trust, respect, and camaraderie. By the end of the year, the trainers had developed both skills in training delivery and confidence in the curriculum. In early April 2003, prior to the beginning of the final class for the fiscal year, another debriefing was held at the University of Washington. The room was equipped with a computer, projector, and Internet access so that online materials could be viewed. Two trainers from eastern Washington participated via conference call.

The number one concern that trainers heard was that learners were devoting excessive time to the class, especially to the required readings. Two or three particularly zealous participants appeared to skew the norm, but the trainers agreed that limiting the required readings to one per week—specifically relevant to the week's discussion topic—was in order. In addition, it was recommended that the web pages be reorganized with the required reading listed first, followed by activities and assignments. Recommended readings should be relegated to last place on the page. Because of the volume of postings to DIG_REF, it was suggested that some options be offered for subscribing on either a full or digest basis, along with other ways to manage voluminous discussion lists. Another website revision related to changing the formatting to reflect that the First Week page was actually "orientation." The First Week page should contain only the readings and assignments that follow the orientation session.

The project coordinator reported on the successful all-staff training day at City University, during which learners who had participated in VRS training shared their experiences with colleagues (see next section). This kind of activity was seen as highly desirable, since it extends the training beyond the limited Anytime, Anywhere Answers classes. Developing a template for future use was given a high priority.

A lengthy discussion about problems associated with the instant messaging software ensued. The specific learning objective of the orientation day activity was reiterated—the exposure of participants to the most-used form of online chat communication. The importance of understanding the kind of experiences customers bring to the virtual reference transaction was stressed. Nonetheless, the trainers and curriculum developers agreed that the new software download requirement could be onerous, especially given the many different equipment configurations being used by learners at both home and library. One suggestion was that identity-neutral and instant messaging accounts be established prior to orientation for each class, then distributed to learners as needed. Those who already had ID-neutral names should be encouraged to use them. Another recommendation was that the first online chat meeting not use instant messaging, but rather use the 24/7 Reference meeting application for a more free-form session. This could incorporate escorted browsing for demonstration to the learners. It was noted that some intensive work would be required to compile lists of appropriate sites for browsing. The curriculum was designed to limit the amount of customization that trainers needed to develop, but all agreed that some additional work was worthwhile and expressed willingness to do it.

The discussion of this technical problem led to another lengthy talk about problems associated with viewing slide presentations during online chat meetings. Many learners had reported that slides were not visible at all or only intermittently. The computer and projector were used to demonstrate both the operator and learner views of a presentation. Several different suggestions were made, but no real solution was obvious. The curriculum developers would discuss the problem with the vendor. (A telephone call took place the following day that clarified understanding of the way the software works and also provided a preferred method for pushing slides.) In addition, the scripted questions that were automatically pushed with the slides were critiqued. Several observed that they tended to interrupt the flow of chat, and that they were too long and formally phrased. One possibility would be to develop shorter, more casual messages that could be pushed when trainers think they are needed.

There was insufficient time to implement many of these modifications prior to the beginning of the next class. However, many improvements were implemented when new classes began in fall 2003. This meeting of trainers was both successful and practical. The ongoing commitment to high-quality training was apparent.

TAKING TRAINING BACK

Several librarians from City University participated in VRS training classes, and in spring 2003 their library director decided to devote the annual Staff In-Service Day to a workshop on virtual reference. The library currently provided an active e-mail reference service to its extensive distance-learning student enrollment. The day began with a strategic planning session, but the rest of the day was devoted to the workshop. Staff members who were graduates of the Anytime, Anywhere Answers program planned the day, which included a variety of presentations and activities. The first hour introduced chat reference, covering some of the training basics. The staff paired for simulated virtual reference sessions using computers stationed around the library. There was a nice mix of those familiar with virtual reference and those for whom it was completely new, and there was the usual assortment of technical problems. A one-page "Testing Chat Service" instruction sheet was provided that outlined the respective roles of librarian and patron and offered tips for online transactions. There was much interest and enthusiasm in the exercise. This demonstration formed the basis for the discussions that followed.

In the half hour following this, the group discussed and generated scripts that might be useful for City University library staff to deliver virtual reference service. This was an interesting extension of training to address specific local needs. One hour in the afternoon was devoted to a presentation on "Excellence in Chat Reference." Core competencies were reviewed and several handouts were discussed, including the RUSA guidelines, observations on the challenges of digital reference gleaned from the DIG_REF discussion list, and "chatspeak" terms. A bibliography of readings taken from the training class materials was also included. Another hour provided a variation on the Secret Patron and Virtual Field Trip exercises. Staff members went online to explore local library virtual reference services, choosing from a printed list of URLs, and then critiqued the discovery experience. A paper titled "Discover Chat Service at the Web Pages" summarized many of the questions used to evaluate Anytime, Anywhere

Answers assignments. The final activity of the day was transcript evaluation. Transcripts used in VRS training classes (see appendix B) were distributed and analyzed. A final half hour for impressions, fears, and ideas ended the day.

The City University workshop was an excellent way for training participants to share what they learned with colleagues and also to reinforce their own learning by organizing the workshop, presenting concepts, and beginning customization for local library use.

CONSULTING WITH OTHERS

Throughout the first year of VRS training, there were many opportunities to share experiences, elicit suggestions, and discuss future options with staff members at various libraries and the VRS Steering Committee. In some cases, orientation sessions offered a chance for library administrators or managers not involved in virtual reference to drop in and observe training in progress. While much of this was captured informally and gradually incorporated into the training program, one notable session was the interim report of progress made at the VRS Steering Committee meeting in March 2003. By that time, the value of the learner-produced reports, the chat meeting transcripts, and the evaluation materials was becoming clear. The training had much wider application than originally was expected.

Two shorter variations on the full training curriculum were suggested. The first was a half-day introductory workshop for directors, reference managers, and other staff members from libraries considering the implementation of virtual reference service. This was seen as a combination of presentation and demonstration—Virtual Reference 101. Topics could include an overview of service possibilities and benefits, technical and training requirements, service scope and limitations, marketing considerations, and related issues.

A second workshop, also envisioned as a half-day event, would cover some of the same topics for a different audience: library staff members. VRS training classes uncovered the need to present virtual reference basics to the many library workers who are unfamiliar with live, online digital reference. Demonstrating the way the service works, who it can serve, and benefits like information literacy instruction makes it understandable and useful. There is a need to demystify virtual reference and place it firmly in the realm of reference service rather than as a faddish add-on.

These workshops will be presented in spring 2004.

CONSEQUENCES

The VRS training program had unexpected consequences, especially in terms of evaluating current services. From observing library web pages to participating in live, online digital reference, the tools used by learners to critique the ways in which libraries present and implement public services resulted in both surprising and thoughtful observations. There is much here to consider. In many cases, library staff members seem woefully unprepared to handle online transactions. Learners who participated in Secret Patron scenarios and Virtual Field

Trips encountered many disappointing experiences. The explanation may lie in the "deer in the headlights" syndrome, a mismatch of personal characteristics with service needs, flawed or incomplete technology, inadequate experience and training, lack of administrative support, or a combination of factors. Library staff members who provided virtual reference service rarely clarified questions or offered any description of pushed web pages, and they often left long unexplained lapses while customers waited. It is possible, even probable, that library staff who participated in VRS training are more critical of these transactions than customers would be, but the problems should not be underestimated.

The fact that few libraries do a good job of marketing their services, especially online, has other implications. If few customers use the service, it is unlikely that the inadequacies will be shared. Both good and bad consumer experiences spread by word of mouth. Unfortunately, lack of use by customers also means lack of practice by providers. For Anytime, Anywhere Answers participants, it was easy to spot library staff who were experienced and at ease. They offered the best-quality service.

Many of the tools used for training are equally valuable for assessing library service. Any library could use a variation of the Secret Patron activity to evaluate transactions. The checklists offered in the appendixes provide areas in which many aspects of service can be assessed.

Administrators and supervisors must be open to both comments and criticism in order to take advantage of the opportunities provided by this training. The value of user-oriented activities, in which library staff members experience the other side of service, cannot be overestimated. Who said what to whom is not nearly as interesting as how it was said. Did the staff member take time to clarify the question? Did he or she provide interim indications that someone was still attentive on the library end? Was the transaction personal, using a staff persona and the customer's name when possible? Was the sign-off cordial, inviting return and offering additional help if needed? Even these questions beg the idea that appropriate, authoritative information was transferred. If high-quality customer service is the goal, the results of this training highlight the need for close examination of needed skills and their application in reference service—via any delivery method.

There are many opportunities presented by digital reference service. We can reach out to new customers, provide an ever-widening range of high-quality information, explore more efficient and effective technologies, and create heightened respect for libraries and the services they offer.

APPENDIX

Assessment Tools

INTERNET REFERENCE COMPETENCIES

I AM ABLE TO:	No	Sort of	Yes	Easily
1. Quickly find authoritative online definitions for Internet terms such as TCP/IP.				
2. Briefly explain what Usenet is.				
3. Find and search Usenet newsgroups.				
4. Explain how to download and install Acrobat Reader.				
5. Identify and subscribe to an e-mail list (discussion list) on a specific library-related topic.				
6. Break a URL into its component parts and explain each one.				
7. Determine the origin of a non-U.S. website by identifying the country code in the URL.				
8. Do a "who is" search to find out who registered a specific domain name.				
9. Effectively search web directories such as Yahoo and Librarian's Index to the Internet, using categories and subcategories, and the advanced search features.				
10. Distinguish between effective and ineffective keywords to use in a search engine, such as Google, and in a directory, such as Yahoo.				
11. Translate a reference question into a search engine query, using phrases, truncation, and implied Boolean (+, -).				
12. Use menus to create a Boolean search query in a search engine like HotBot.				
13. Create a complex search query in AltaVista, using Boolean operators, nested expressions, and domain field limiting.				

(Cont'd)

Internet Reference Competencies (Cont'd)

I AM ABLE TO:	No	Sort of	Yes	Easily
14. Find a PowerPoint presentation on a web page using a file-type search.				
15. Explain "on the page" and "off the page" relevancy ranking.				
16. Define "Invisible Web" and explain the types of files not found by search engines.				
17. Name two directories of Invisible Web databases.				
18. Copy and paste text or graphics from a web page into Word or PowerPoint files.				
19. Identify common file formats (.html, .txt, .pdf, .jpeg, .zip, .mp3, .mpeg).				
20. Quickly find the full text of Supreme Court decisions.				
21. Quickly locate ready reference sources on the Web (e.g., online calendars, currency converters, etc.).				
22. Show a parent how to find age-appropriate websites for elementary school assignments.				
23. Locate and change web browser preferences for start page, font size, and background color.				
24. View the source code of a web page, identifying the title field and image captions.				
25. Show a library patron which California newspapers have online archives.				
26. Locate the lyrics and sound files for national anthems.				
27. Find a photograph of someone who is in the news today.				
28. Quickly find high-quality reproductions of works by well-known artists.				
29. Choose the most effective starting point for a search (directory, search engine, guide site, searchable database).				
30. Quickly and accurately locate official home pages for city, state, federal, and foreign government agencies.				
31. Locate online business newspapers for Washington State.				
32. Locate statistical resources for Latin American countries.				
33. Define "webring" and show examples of several webrings.				
34. Define "weblog" and find several library-related weblogs.				
35. Evaluate websites for authority, reliability, and currency.				
36. Identify two reliable online sources of information on search engines.				

WINDOWS MULTITASKING COMPETENCIES

I AM ABLE TO:	No	Sort of	Yes	Easily
1. Use the Windows keyboard commands for Select All, Copy, and Paste.				
2. Use ALT + TAB to move between open windows.				
3. Use the Windows logo key to get to the Start Menu, Windows Desktop, and Windows Explorer.				
4. Install and use the Google Toolbar.				
5. Use the Ctrl and Shift keys to highlight multiple items in a drop-down menu.				
6. Adjust monitor display resolution to maximize your "desktop real estate."				
7. Explore search engine results quickly by dragging and dropping links into a second browser window.				
8. Use the keyboard shortcuts (Ctrl + F, Ctrl + N, Ctrl + H) for common browser functions.				
9. Move a web page out of a frame by opening it in a new browser window.				
10. Print specific pages or copy selected text in a PDF document.				
11. Explain to a library user how to download and install Acrobat Reader.				
12. Save a file from a web page to the Desktop.				
13. Clear History files, cache, and Temporary Internet Files.				
14. Create folders in the Internet Explorer Links Toolbar and drag new links into the folders.				

INITIAL SKILLS ASSESSMENT OF COMPETENCIES FOR VIRTUAL REFERENCE

The effective delivery of virtual reference services depends on a range of skills and abilities. Some are basic reference skills, while other skills are unique to virtual reference. Circle the number that best indicates your confidence in your current ability to demonstrate each skill (1 is not confident, 7 is completely confident).

1 = Not Confident 7 = Completely Confident

1. Communicate clearly, effectively, and professionally in a chat reference transaction, creating and using pre-scripted messages when appropriate.

   1 2 3 4 5 6 7

2. Conduct an effective reference interview in a chat environment, clarifying the patron's question before searching.

   1 2 3 4 5 6 7

3. Search the Internet quickly and efficiently, choosing the best starting points for answering the patron's question.

   1 2 3 4 5 6 7

4. Effectively search, and demonstrate searching of your library databases. Explain any restrictions or technical problems connected with the use of library databases.

   1 2 3 4 5 6 7

5. During a virtual reference transaction, assist users in applying critical thinking skills to locating, using, and evaluating information on the Internet.

   1 2 3 4 5 6 7

6. Effectively guide a patron through a collaborative browsing session, explaining the search step-by-step.

   1 2 3 4 5 6 7

7. Evaluate your own virtual reference transcripts, as well as those of your colleagues, and identify improvement strategies.

   1 2 3 4 5 6 7

8. Manage multiple windows and quickly use Windows keyboard commands and appropriate shortcuts.

   1 2 3 4 5 6 7

9. Troubleshoot technical problems and clearly explain technical problems to the patron.

   1 2 3 4 5 6 7

10. Create and apply reference transaction policies in an online environment (e.g., scope of service, time limits, harassment, etc.).

    1 2 3 4 5 6 7

11. Identify resources for continuous upgrading of web-searching skills and improvement of skills in all areas of reference services.

    1 2 3 4 5 6 7

FOLLOW-UP SKILLS ASSESSMENT (SECTION 2)
(Questions Added to Initial Skills Assessment)

1. Are you using the skills taught in the training on the job?

   YES NO

   If YES, please circle your estimate of the percentage of the skills you are using:

   10–25% 25–50% 50–75% 100%

2. Do you have indications from your customers that your approach to offering virtual reference service improved as a result of the training?

   YES NO

   If YES, how has it improved? (Check all that apply.)

   ____ Communicate effectively throughout a virtual reference transaction

   ____ Provide a wider range of resources, both online and print

   ____ Provide more relevant and/or accurate information

   ____ Use chat format confidently

   ____ Provide guidance in searching and evaluation (information literacy)

   ____ Ensure customer received needed information

   ____ Other

3. Do supervisors and/or colleagues indicate that your library benefited from your participation in the training?

   YES NO

   If YES, how has it benefited? (Check all that apply.)

   ____ Greater customer satisfaction

   ____ Skills shared with colleagues

   ____ More effective reference service

   ____ Improved procedures or policies

   ____ Improved web page interface for virtual reference service

   ____ Other

4. Please add any comments or suggestions:

EVALUATION OF TRAINING

Goals for the training—were they met?	*High* 5	4	3	2	1	*Low* 0
1. The content was logical, organized, and presented clearly on the web pages and in the handouts.						
2. The readings, activities, and assignments facilitated the acquisition of skills for virtual reference.						
3. The training emphasized exploration, discovery, and reflection on key concepts in virtual reference services.						
4. The trainers were supportive and responsive to individual learning needs.						
5. Overall, my rating of this training is:						

Objectives for the learners—were they met?	5	4	3	2	1	0
After the training, I am able to:						
1. Identify current-awareness resources for virtual reference.						
2. Conduct an effective reference interview using chat.						
3. Identify the policies and procedures needed for a new virtual reference service.						
4. Use virtual reference transcripts as tools for service improvement.						
5. Introduce information literacy skills to patrons in virtual reference transactions.						

In this training what was most beneficial to you?

What areas do you think could be improved?

Any additional comments and suggestions?

APPENDIX

B Transcripts

The following selections from transcripts reviewed by Anytime, Anywhere Answers class members have been edited to remove information that identifies individuals and institutions. All of these were developed from actual university and public library virtual reference transaction transcripts and were intended to illustrate a variety of interactions, both good and bad. The guidelines used to evaluate them are reproduced at the end of the appendix.

TRANSCRIPT 1
Helping with Homework (Public Library)

Patron: What is the Slave/African American culture?

Librarian: Please hold while I take a moment to examine your request.

Librarian: Hi. May I ask if you are a student? If you are what grade are you in?

Librarian: I'm not sure I understand your question. Can you explain more specifically what you are looking for?

Patron: what are some things that the slaves in the cotton fields would do.

Librarian: OK, so you want to know about the work they did in the cotton fields?

Patron: No, more like traditions . . . songs or dances.

Librarian: OK, what grade are you in?

Patron: 8th.

Librarian: OK, I will look for some information for you. This will take a few minutes.

Librarian: Here is a website that has some examples of slave songs. I will push the page to you now.

[Item sent: "Slave Songs of the United States"]

Patron: OK, thanx this works.

Librarian: OK, is that all you need?

Patron: Yeah.

Librarian: OK, bye.

[User has closed the session]

TRANSCRIPT 2
Citing the Source (Public Library)

Patron: Describe 5 ways that God demonstrated God's saving love and power during Moses' life.

Librarian: Hold on and I'll see what I can find . . .

Patron: OK

Librarian: Well . . . he showed his power by sending the plagues to Egypt, opening the Red Sea so the Israelites could escape,

Librarian: He also made a covenant with Moses by giving him the 10 commandments . . . that kind of stuff?

Patron: Yup, that stuff.

Librarian: He punished the golden calf worshipers with a bolt of lightening, and he finally led the Israelites to the Promised Land.

Librarian: Does that work for you? Anything else?

Patron: hmm, let me think. That works for me . . . by any chance you have the scripture references for these events?

Librarian: Not the specific references, but you should be able to find them all in Exodus 3-36.

Patron: OK

Librarian: It's pretty easy to track them down with the section headings . . . good luck.

Patron: thanks

[Librarian has closed the session]

Patron: one last question . . .

TRANSCRIPT 3
Other Relevant Sources (Public Library)

Patron: Okay, so I am doing this debate in my English class about cell phone safety, and its role in car accidents and links to cancer. I'm supposed to prove that it isn't a major contributing cause of car accidents, and am looking for some articles or sources that will help me give a strong debate. Is there any websites, etc. that you could please direct me to?

Librarian: Please hold while I take a moment to examine your request.

Librarian: I will now search for that information.

[Item sent: Web page—"Ban Cell Phones in Cars?" (Commentary)]

[Item sent: Web page—"Cell Phone Use while Driving Increases Crash Risk"]

[Item sent: Web page—"Should Using a Cell Phone while Driving Be Illegal?"]

Librarian: I did a Google search and sent you three pages. Did you receive them?

Patron: Yes, I did. I think these articles are great and I can start to draw an argument from them. Thank you very much!

Librarian: You are welcome. Is there anything else?

Patron: No, that is all. Thanks again.

(User has disconnected)

TRANSCRIPT 4
Giving Opinions (Public Library)

Patron: If a car is crunched into a compact cube does its mass change?

Librarian: Please hold while I take a moment to examine your request.

Librarian: Hi, I'll start looking at your question. My first instinct tells me no, aside from the glass that would fall out. But I'll try to find some information. Tough question!

[Item sent: Web page—"Explanation of Weight and Mass"]

Librarian: This website states that mass is the amount of matter in an object. Compressing that matter shouldn't affect the mass.

Librarian: "Mass is the amount of matter in an object. It has no direction associated with it. Mass stays the same no matter what force is acting on the object."

Patron: OK, thank you.

Librarian: Like I said, you might lose some glass from the car, but otherwise, you shouldn't lose any mass. Does that answer your question?

Patron: Ya, thank you bye.

(User has closed the session)

TRANSCRIPT 5
Suggesting Print Materials (University Library)

Patron: Need info on Hawaiian shirt patterns.

Please hold, a librarian will be with you shortly.

Librarian: Hello! Welcome to the (Virtual Reference) service. My name is . . .

Librarian: What information do you need? Do you need more than the pattern itself?

Patron: I'm in a pop culture class and would like to investigate whether Hawaiian shirts accurately reflect or distort Hawaiian culture.

Librarian: There is a book called *The Aloha Shirt: Spirit of the Islands* / Dale Hope with Gregory Tozian. Is this the type of information you are looking for?

Librarian: If you are a student, faculty or staff, I can explain how you can request this item. If you use a public library, let me know which system, and I can find out if it's available.

Librarian: I think this is the book for you. Do you have a library card?

Patron: I am a student. That book sounds great—but, doesn't this library have it?

Librarian: No, but I can show you how to request it from (another university) if you have a minute.

Patron: Great!

[Here the Librarian demonstrates how to search the library catalog, shows the search strategy, then takes the patron to the combined catalog for all four-year colleges in ________________. Then shows patron how to request the book from (another university).]

Librarian: Do you have a library PIN number?

Patron: Yeah, I do. I think I can take it from here.

Librarian: Great. Thanks for trying our new service. Would you like to look for journal articles?

Patron: Maybe later. Books will do for now.

Librarian: Bye.

[Patron has disconnected]

[Librarian—user has closed this session]

TRANSCRIPT 6
Clarifying the Question (Public Library)

Patron: I need to find out if Stephanie was a popular name in the 1960s? If not the 1960s, when did it become a popular name?

[A library staff member is coming online . . . please wait.]

Librarian: I'm looking at your question right now. Can you tell me more about what you need?

Patron: I need to know about the popularity of the name Stephanie.

Librarian: Interesting question. I'm going to search some name sites and see if they include any historical information . . .

Librarian: So far, I'm only finding information about what the name means.

Librarian: I understand your question. It's a difficult one. It will take a little time. . . . If you prefer not to wait, I can reply by e-mail . . .

Patron: You don't know any web sources you can go to?

Librarian: Sorry, I won't know until I find it.

Librarian: This site claims to have background meaning on names. Let's have a look.

Patron: I already know the meaning of Stephanie.

Librarian: I understand that you're looking for the history of the popularity of the name; in what decade did it become popular.

Patron: Is there a place that keeps track of popular names throughout history?

Librarian: I don't know of such a place; I'm looking for one.

Librarian: Here's one on regional (but not historical) popularity.

Librarian: [Item sent—"Popularity of Names in Regions of the U.S."] http://interoz.com/usr/bethed/nation.htm

Patron: This is not very detailed.

Librarian: I think I may have to consult some databases and print material. Is it OK if I e-mail you back? If so, will you verify your e-mail address please?

Patron: That would be fine. I would think that some government document site would have this info. But I will wait for your e-mail.

Librarian: And do you have a deadline for the information?

Patron: My e-mail is __________________ . No deadline.

Librarian: Thank you for using the _______________. A complete transcript, including web links, will be sent to your e-mail address.

[Patron has disconnected]

Here is the follow-up e-mail:

From:
To: (E-mail address)
Subject: history of the popularity of the name Stephanie

Dear _______,
You were correct in thinking of government documents as the most authoritative source of information on this topic. The trick was figuring out the right phrase to search: "popular baby names," which is what the federal and state governments all seem to use for information related to your question. The Social Security Administration tracks the national data. All the links you need are at: http://www.ssa.gov/OACT/NOTES/note139/note139.html.

I'll let you investigate the details, but I can tell you that Stephanie didn't make the top ten list until 1973. It has stayed on the list pretty regularly through 1992, and is still on the top 100 list (for 2001), ranked 37th. As your initial question was about the 1960s, don't miss the link to "Top 1,000 names of the 1960s." Stephanie is ranked 45th for that entire decade. According to *American Given Names: Their Origin and History in the Context of the English Language* by George R. Stewart (New York : Oxford University Press, 1979), the name Stephanie did not gain popularity until the mid-twentieth century. With regard to the early history of the name, according to the *History of Christian Names* (Detroit, republished by Gale Research Co., 1966), the feminine form of Stephen (Stephanie) was used "at least as early as the thirteenth century."

Thanks for using the ______________.

GUIDELINES FOR EVALUATING TRANSCRIPTS

Read the chat reference transcripts that the trainers e-mail to you. Keep in mind the behaviors that are effective in face-to-face or telephone reference. Do these behaviors appear in the transcripts? Summarize your impressions of the transcripts, using these questions to guide you in writing your summary. Post your summary to the VRS training online discussion list.

What are your overall impressions of the service that the patrons received?

Which of the transactions did you think was the most effective? Least effective? Why?

What positive feedback would you give to the staff providing the service? What improvements would you suggest?

Were there any opportunities for information literacy instruction? Did the librarians use these opportunities?

What do you see that you want to remember when you are providing virtual reference services?

How will you use the transcripts from your virtual reference service as tools for improvement?

APPENDIX

Virtual Field Trip Reports

VIRTUAL FIELD TRIP QUESTIONS

Site visited: ____

Date / Time: ______________________________

Branding

What is the name of the service?

What image or logo is used to "brand" the service?

How is the service described? Is library jargon used?

Do you think the name, image, and description are appealing and attention-getting?

Is the link easy to find on the main library web page?

Are there links to the virtual reference service from all areas of the library's website? From the catalog? From the online databases? From the circulation information page?

Accessibility

Is the service open to anyone?

Is a library card or student ID number required for access?

What other restrictions exist? Where are these restrictions stated?

Is an e-mail address required or recommended? If not required, is it clear how the user will receive a transcript of the transaction?

When is the real-time reference service open? What are the user's options when the service is closed? Is the service available on holidays?

Scope of Service

Is there a clear statement about the kinds of questions that are appropriate for this real-time reference service? Does it offer more than simple, factual answers?

If targeted to college students, is it clear how much research help will be provided?

Does the service promote information literacy by offering to demonstrate how to find answers or use the Web more effectively?

Are links to starting points for web searching provided? Links to how to cite web sources?

Authority

Who are the staff providing answers through this service? What are their qualifications? Subject expertise?

Is there any disclaimer about providing medical or legal advice?

Are there any statements about copyright restrictions or about citing online sources?

Confidentiality and Data Gathered

What kind of information is gathered in advance about the user or about the question? Reading level or level of information sought? Homework assignment?

Phone number? How is this information used?

What is the privacy or confidentiality policy?

Where can a user find the privacy policy?

Is there an option to remain anonymous? If so, is there an explanation of what that option means?

General Impressions

Some things that I want to remember for planning and implementing our virtual reference service are:

APPENDIX

Secret Patron Scenarios

No activity provided more compelling and useful experience than the Secret Patron exercise. The scenarios were developed from transcripts of actual virtual reference transactions in both academic and public library settings. The first example includes a copy of the actual transcript from which it was developed. The checklist provided for use in evaluating transactions follows the scenarios.

SCENARIO A

You Are:

A 50-year-old man who teaches Spanish to high school students in suburban Seattle. You have an old, worn-out dictionary that you think is the best one available for students learning to speak Spanish. You want to buy more copies of it for your students. On the reverse side of the title page, it says "This new Dover edition first published in 1958 is an unabridged republication of the War Department Technical Manual TM 30-900, Dictionary of Spoken Spanish."

Your Approach to Asking a Question Is:

You tend to phrase a question in the way that makes sense to you. You haven't used chat before so you make a few mistakes and hit the ENTER key too quickly, in the middle of a sentence.

You Start With:

Where can I find an old (1940s) government document

Then You Add:

It is War Dept. Manual TM 30-900

Transcript for Scenario A

Patron: Where can I find an old (1940s) government document

A librarian will be with you in about a minute.

[A Librarian has joined the session]

Librarian 1: I need a little more information in order to help you find the answer. Can you tell me more?

Patron: It is War Dept. manual TM 30-900

Librarian 1: [Page sent—"State and Local Government Web Sites"]

Librarian 1: The library won't have that kind of thing in-house, but you can search some of these links online.

Librarian 1: I have a feeling that you will probably have go to the Regional National Archives facility for that as well.

Librarian: http://www.archives.gov/facilities/wa/seattle.html

Patron: This is a federal gov document from before Dept of Defense was formed, not local gov.

Librarian 1: Pacific Alaska Region (Seattle) maintains retired records from Federal agencies and courts in Idaho, Oregon, and Washington.

Librarian 1: Please contact the NAR for further help.

Librarian 1: I need to help other patrons waiting, a transcript of this session will be e-mailed to you with all the links we visited. Thanks for using _______________!

Librarian 1: note to staff: COMP

(Patron tries again to get more help)

Patron: Dear _______________, We got disconnected. I was replying that the Federal archive sight in Seattle would probably not have this kind of doc. Is there a gov printing office that could reproduce it?

A librarian will be with you in about a minute.

[A Librarian has joined the session]

Librarian 2: Hello, this is the reference librarian. I'm reading your question . . .

Librarian 2: It looks like another librarian had been helping you.

Librarian 2: Let me review what took place in your previous session. Just a moment, please.

Librarian 2: I'm having trouble finding your transcript. Can you recap your question for me?

Patron: I'm looking for War dept Manual TM 30-900 from 1940's

Librarian 2: What is this manual about?

Librarian 2: Is it current?

Patron: It is actually a unique Spanish dictionary. It was republished in 50s by Dover.

Librarian 2: Do you need that exact publication or will anything else work?

Patron: Since Dover published it, someone else may have, but I would like that doc. i.e. dictionary.

Librarian 2: This may be hard to track down . . .

Librarian 2: Can we look into this more and get back to you by e-mail?

Patron: Would it be helpful to know that Dover gave it a different title?

Librarian 2: Yes, what is that title?

Librarian 2: Any and all information you have on this is useful.

Patron: Dictionary of Spoken Spanish. It says Lib of Congress Card Catalog 58-14487

Librarian 2: Okay, thanks, let me check on that

Librarian 2: The only libraries which show owning this publication are in CA . . .

Librarian 2: You will need to have your local library borrow this book through interlibrary loan.

Patron: Thank you. You've been helpful!

Patron: Are you able to check other WA libraries? Seattle?

Librarian 2: I am looking at a catalog of libraries worldwide

Patron: How about purchase?

Librarian 2: I don't know how you would purchase something so old, without going to a used bookseller . . .

(Time lapse of about two minutes)

Patron: Are we finished? Do you have other thoughts?

Librarian 2: I think the easiest route would be to go through your local libraries' interlibrary loan

Patron: Thanks very much.

Librarian 2: Your welcome.

Librarian 2: If you need further assistance, please feel free to contact us again. Thank you for using the _____________ Service. Goodbye!

[Patron has disconnected]

[Librarian 2—user has closed this session]

SCENARIO B

You Are:

A community college student doing a Zoology paper that is due tomorrow. You don't have time to go to the library and you just need a few facts to add to the paper. An e-mail answer is OK if you can have it by tonight. You have already checked an encyclopedia, a few websites, and a few books.

Your Approach to Asking a Question Is:

Short and to the point. You need just this information to complete your paper. You are an experienced chat user so you tend to give short quick responses with minimal capitalization and punctuation.

You Start With:

does the okapi give birth while standing up?

Then You Ask:

how big are the baby okapi? is gestation like giraffes?

SCENARIO C

You Are:

An elderly woman who recently learned about the death of a friend in California. Your friend died almost two years ago. You don't know where your friend is buried but would like to visit her grave while you are in Los Angeles next week. You don't know where you could get this information. You have lost all contact with your friend's family.

Your Approach to Asking a Question Is:

Quite formal and polite. You use e-mail but haven't used chat before so you tend to hit the ENTER key at the wrong time.

You Start With:

Are there online cemetery records?

Then You Say:

I want to know where a friend of mine was interred. I want to visit her grave if that's possible. Thank you.

SCENARIO D

You Are:

A 9th grade student with an English Literature paper due tomorrow. You need to compare three different versions of the Cinderella fairy tale. You are not really sure what the teacher wants, what kind of comparison to write, or whether you need to compare different translations or different versions. It would be great if the librarian can help you clarify the assignment.

Your Approach to Asking a Question Is:

You don't use correct spelling, punctuation, and capitalization. You are an avid chat user and quite familiar with the lingo.

You Start With:

i need diffen vertions of cinderella for h/w . . . i need it asap. . . . PLEASE! i need anythng . . . i hav 0 . . . !?

SCENARIO E

You Are:

A young man who received a ticket when you made a right turn from the left lane of a busy street. A friend of yours told you about how he got out of paying a traffic ticket because he went to court and the police officer who issued the ticket didn't show up. This ticket will severely impact your insurance costs so you want to get it dismissed.

Your Approach to Asking a Question Is:

Informal. You haven't used a library except for homework while you were in school. You don't know the correct way to express your question but you really want to get this ticket erased from your driving record.

You Start With:

how can I get out of a ticket??

Then You Say:

I really need to get out of this because it will make my insurance go up

SCENARIO F

You Are:

An older man who is doing some financial planning. You have a very traditional marriage—you control all the finances, your wife controls the household. Your credit card is in your name only.

Your Approach to Asking a Question Is:

You haven't used chat before so you make a few mistakes and hit the ENTER key too quickly, in the middle of a sentence. You use upper/lower case and punctuation.

You Start With:

If I die, does my wife have to pay my credit card bills?

They You Say:

Her name has never been on my credit cards.

SCENARIO G

You Are:

A 65-year-old woman who has persistent pain in her foot and hasn't gotten a lot of help from her doctor.

Your Approach to Asking a Question Is:

Very formal, using correct spelling, punctuation, and capitalization. You want to complain about your doctor and how unsympathetic he has been. You haven't used the Internet much except for e-mail to your grandchildren, but want to learn how to use it to find information.

You Start With:

What is the real name for heel spurs?

They You Say:

How can I find medical advice? I want some advice for getting rid of the pain in my heel. I have been wearing orthotics but they don't help.

SCENARIO H

You Are:

A college student working on a paper for your American Studies class. You want to show that the U.S. is the most inventive nation in the world. You think that a good way to prove this is by the number of patents issued in the U.S. compared to the number issued in other countries. You want the latest figures.

Your Approach to Asking a Question Is:

Informal, using minimal punctuation. You are familiar with chat expressions. You will need to cite your sources so you want to see the most authoritative and current ones. You also want to know how to cite a web page in a bibliography.

You Start With:

What is the total # of U.S. patents issued as of Dec 31 2002 . . . total # granted in other countries, same date?

Then You Say:

Is this the most reputable source . . . how do I list a website in my bibliography?

CHECKLIST FOR EVALUATING SECRET PATRON TRANSACTIONS

1. Setting the Tone
   ____ The librarian greeted me personally and used my name
   ____ It was clear that he/she was interested in my query and ready to provide assistance
2. Getting the Question Straight
   The librarian clarified my question using:
   ____ An open probe
   ____ A closed probe
   ____ Both open and closed probes
   ____ Did not clarify my question
3. Keeping Me Informed
   ____ He/she asked me whether I wanted to see how to find the answer
   ____ The librarian's responses were clear, easy to read, and free of library jargon
   ____ The librarian kept me informed about his/her progress in finding an answer, providing a time estimate when needed
   ____ He or she let me know what he was doing—e.g., still looking, pushing a web page, escorting, etc.
   ____ The librarian provided help with any technical difficulties
4. Providing Information
   ____ He/she identified authoritative information appropriate for my need and interest
   ____ The librarian gave me time to determine whether the information found actually answered my question to my satisfaction. Didn't rush me by pushing too much information.
   ____ Cited the source of the information
   ____ Asked if I wanted to be shown more sources
   ____ Recognized if my question needed to be referred elsewhere or could be more effectively answered through e-mail
5. Follow-up
   ____ Asked if the information found answered my question to my satisfaction
   ____ Asked if I had any other questions
   ____ Encouraged me to use the service again
   ____ Thanked me
   ____ I was asked to evaluate my experience with the service
   ____ My other comments about the reference transaction are. . .

APPENDIX

Policies and Procedures

A checklist was provided as an evaluation tool for examining online library policies and procedures. Following the checklist are selected reports from learners who compared and contrasted a variety of these documents that covered both staff and user expectations.

POLICIES AND PROCEDURES: The Nuts and Bolts of Virtual Reference

One of your challenges in establishing a virtual reference service is the development of guidelines—all of the policies and procedures that form the foundation for your new service. Real-time chat reference differs from in-person reference and even from e-mail reference. The policies that your library created for these other modes of reference do not necessarily apply to a chat reference environment. Here are some of the questions that your policies and procedures may need to address.

Setting up the Service

How will users be involved in shaping the service?

What kind of a team will you need to assemble for decision making and coordination? Who will be responsible for technical problems? Database licensing issues? Creating and maintaining scripts?

Where will the staff providing the service be located? If librarians are also working at a public reference desk, how will you handle serving both in-person and virtual patrons? Will librarians work from home?

Scope of Service

Who may use this virtual reference service? If a library card or student ID is required, how will you authenticate the user?

What types of questions are appropriate? Do you need a disclaimer about medical or legal questions?

How will you handle frequently asked questions? Alert colleagues to repetitive questions (e.g., homework assignments)?

Evaluation

What are your goals for this new service?

What types of data will you collect to measure progress toward these goals?

How will you evaluate the cost of the service?

What data are needed to demonstrate its impact?

Virtual Collections

Will you create a web page of starting points, links to databases, recommended web resources, etc., for the staff providing virtual reference?

Referral of Questions and Follow-up

How will questions be referred to another librarian or to a subject expert?

What about telephone callback or e-mail follow-up? Patrons with undeliverable e-mail addresses?

How will you handle specific questions about circulation issues or ILL?

Staffing

How many people will be needed to staff the new service? (Preferred Solutions provides a Workforce Calculator for staffing a call center.)

Who will you choose? Will librarians be the only ones answering questions? What about trained paraprofessionals or students?

Should real names be used by the staff?

Who will coordinate the scheduling of staff?

Hours of Availability

When will the service be available? Holidays? Will the hours of service vary during the academic year?

Databases and Document Delivery

Are there any licensing issues connected with the library's proprietary databases? Authentication issues?

How will you deliver print materials to the patron? Will a scanner or fax machine be available?

Administration

Who will administer the service? What is that person's role? Does this person supervise the staff providing the service?

Who has access to the transcripts? Who reviews the transcripts? Do you want peer review?

What mechanisms will you set up for staff to share experiences, and to clarify and refine your policies and procedures?

Confidentiality

Will any identifying information be connected to the transcripts?

If using transcripts for evaluation and training purposes, how will you ensure the privacy of the users? How will you communicate your privacy policy to users?

Patron Conduct

How will you handle harassment, inappropriate language, rudeness, misuse of the service, etc.? Will you deny service to anyone who violates your rules of conduct?

Will you establish any limits on the number of questions? Time limits?

Time to Explore

1. Use the Policies and Procedures for Virtual Reference tables.
2. Select three examples from each section (Service Overview for Users, Examples of Privacy Statements, Guidelines for Staff) to review.
3. Use the note-taking form to record your impressions and relevant examples.
4. Summarize your thoughts on policies and procedures for virtual reference service and post your summary to the VRS Training discussion list.

APPENDIX F

Online Meeting Transcript

The following transcript is the result of an online meeting conducted for a spring 2003 VRS training class. It has been edited for clarity and to remove identifying information. Although some amusing comments are included, most irrelevant exchanges have been removed, as have URLs for slides and web pages. While the original capitalization has been retained, spelling has been corrected and, in some cases, words added to ensure that phrases make sense.

This transcript is an excellent example of the kind of familiarity and group chemistry that can evolve over a five-week, blended learning course. It also demonstrates the kind of insights, thoughtful comments, and suggestions that characterized most of the online meetings, as well as the good humor. The participants represented a mix of public and academic libraries; one was a library school student. One trainer was a university librarian, the other worked at a large public library.

Online meetings utilized 24/7 Reference software. Both trainers and learners automatically received a copy of the complete transcript, which included URLs for all web pages visited and slides displayed.

The topic for this meeting was marketing virtual reference services. A prepared set of slides was used to guide the discussion, and a variety of web pages that illustrated various aspects of branding and service elements were pushed to participants.

Daria: (Trainer) Welcome, the meeting will be starting soon. What you are looking at is a web page—not a powerpoint slide. [Public Library System website: "Marketing Ideas for Libraries"]

Linda: I have donut and tea in hand and am ready for anything. Will there be a powerpoint presentation this morning?

Daria: Yes, a mixture of powerpoint and web pages.

Nancy: (Trainer) This looks like a cool site, Daria.

Daria: Today we are focusing on the many aspects of marketing your library's virtual reference services. [slide sent: Definition of marketing]

Daria: "marketing links the organizations with its environment" is the slide

Daria: what do you think about this quote?

Barbara: i really dislike the term "marketing"—it sounds so commercial, but i guess it's the best term we have, huh?

Karen: i think it refers to knowing your target audience

Daria: what kind of linkages are being talked about?

Barbara: linkages = users/patrons?

Karen: knowing the age-group, methods of communicating, etc.

Susan: Hard to get used to, but we have so much competition today we aren't the only choice anymore and need to evolve with our patrons

Emily: It reminds us that we can't just do our thing and expect our users to know about and understand our value to them.

Karen: yes, they can go elsewhere otherwise

Linda: the terminology is different but the idea is not

Daria: Let's talk about a big component of marketing—Branding. [slide sent: Branding includes all the associations that a library user makes with the services.]

Karen: is this basically the logo presence?

Daria: Yes. Logos.

Nancy: Karen—it's actually more than the logo

Nancy: it includes what are called "taglines" that describe the service [slide sent: A brand should establish emotional connection with users, communicate the value of the service, provide a distinct identity, function as an education tool.]

Linda: the challenge is getting something that is short & sweet and gives the info needed

Susan: Short info so patron knows exactly what you can deliver sounds like the way to go

Kathy: also something that conveys the idea that the service is new (different?)

Karen: but be careful about using slang terms that have mixed connotations . . .

Susan: We have to clearly identify for ourselves what we offer also

Kawanna: I think a lot of libraries think a logo is enough, that the user will "understand" what the service is

Barbara: or "just what you need"

Kathleen: But brand also includes an attitude, doesn't it? I'm thinking of all the ways car and beer commercials try to convey that they're cool.

Linda: i liked sites that used different fonts & font sizes to catch the eye

Daria: let's look at elements of branding . . . [slide sent: program name - tagline - graphics - program description]

Karen: i think someone mentioned a while back about consistency from site to site

Susan: Appearance is important, if the patron is lost in a messy page, they skip it

Linda: how many patrons go from site to site?

Linda: oh, talking about sites from the same library?

Karen: i mean "ask a librarian" which appeared at several library sites . . . familiarity with term

Nancy: Kathleen's point is good and it might have gotten lost: the emotional appeal

Barbara: "catchy" name particular to library

Linda: ask a librarian isn't exciting

Nancy: I guess the point about consistency across the country is that people know what it is—just like they know what Google is!

Karen: how do you appeal emotionally to library users

Barbara: more and more patrons will understand "ask a . . . " as time goes on

Daria: let's take a look at some brands. [slide sent]

Emily: I've heard that attitude or emotional appeal describe a 'personality' for the service or organization.

Kathleen: Or name chosen to appeal to a certain target group . . . does everyone remember when Kentucky Fried Chicken rebranded themselves as "KFC" because the word "fried" now conveys negative things to younger people?

Kawanna: I like a term that lets you know it is an information source

Daria: What does this site say to you? [Web page sent: Public Library Virtual Reference Service with distinctive brand "nickname"]

Linda: Using Q & A as part of the name is good

Susan: Do we need to be different at the academic level with our branding?

Karen: so, getting beyond the initial nickname takes you to more recognizable 24/7

Kathleen: That [service nickname] sounds like a lot of librarians are trying to be too cute!

Linda: i think academic sites should look different from public libraries

Karen: do you think of your audience as more e-savvy?

Barbara: cute doesn't work in academics . . .

Kawanna: I wonder how many people they lose because the 24/7 isn't on the main page?

Kathy: but they probably attract kids—maybe they want that . . .

Barbara: appealing to the user's attitude about the work does, at least what i've found in academics

Karen: yes, what audience do you want to attract

Kathleen: when I was a kid, that [service nickname] had a definite negative connotation, though—I wonder if it's the same today?

Karen: and as someone said in a previous meeting, are these patrons the people who have been contacting us anyway, in other ways before

Susan: I noticed several sites which didn't make virtual reference very accessible—I wondered if they realized how it was seen by the first time user

Karen: do we want to appeal to a new audience, new methods

Kathleen: I wonder if they focus-group tested the name before rolling it out?

Linda: [Service nickname] would be remembered even if for negative reasons

Barbara: VR might be hidden because the service might not be able to handle all the "new" patrons or is it because they're still "testing"?

Susan: I think VR has to appeal to the audience coming up so we don't lose them completely. Branding can keep us in the picture

Linda: if hidden they won't get enough numbers to make their VR work

Daria: does the [service nickname] communicate the value of the service?

Kathy: they came out pretty big—i think it'd be hard to pull back [service nickname] if it bombs

Kawanna: It still sounds like a children's program to me.

Kathleen: And it will be hard to reposition this for a new target audience without renaming the service and confusing those who already use it.

Barbara: i thought about kids when i saw this the first time

Linda: if you start with children the future is bright

Barbara: would adults take this seriously?

Daria: Let's look at another municipal library. [Web page sent: Multitype Library Consortium Virtual Reference Service]

Karen: i like the visuals on this page

Susan: I would ask—who have they identified as their audience? Is this name supposed to appeal to them?

Daria: What about this brand?

Kathleen: I do like the visuals—I'm lukewarm about [service name], though

Karen: it's a little cluttered logo

Barbara: a little bold—i wanted to step back about five feet and readjust my eyes!

Kathy: unless you're from that area.

Daria: What about the tagline?

Karen: what IS the tagline here

Kawanna: It doesn't say enough—not everyone will know what a consortium is or what the service does.

Barbara: if the public knows what [service name] is

Karen: is the tag the last half of the [service name]?

Susan: Jargon is really not a good idea in taglines

Kathy: looks like a bad URL

Daria: A tagline is something you state you want your audience to identify with. I will show you a QandA tagline later

Karen: yes, URL with numbers and letters

Karen: I like Ask . . .

Daria: Let's go to another consortium. [Web page sent: Multitype Library Consortium Virtual Reference Service]

Kathleen: I remember when the Internet Public Library's virtual reference service rolled out. Their tagline was (maybe still is?) "The day begins at midnight." It didn't clearly convey what the service *did,* but I certainly found it intriguing . . . this one, though, confuses without intrigue

Daria: Look at their tagline.

Kathy: a bit grand, eh?

Daria: The authoritative source for expert information

Barbara: they're proud of their service, obviously

Karen: maybe to distinguish from Google. i like powered by your library

Kathleen: y'know—librarians are hung up on "authoritative"—I don't know if others are . . . but at least the tagline conveys what they're offering

Kathy: not friendly, but reassuring

Barbara: and the "fee or free" heading might scare off potential users

Daria: But they are making a stand about their service.

Kathleen: I actually like the line on the page, "Discover how easy getting the right answer can be," a lot better.

Linda: i do like the colors (i'm going to sites on another window)

Kawanna: I like the "librarians inside" on the open book.

Barbara: could "we" all be a little less pompous?

Kathy: at least they don't say the authoritative answer will be provided RIGHT NOW!!

Daria: This service launched a very successful marketing campaign.

Nancy: I agree—authoritative may mean very little to many people

Kathleen: right, they're making a stand. I'm just not sure it's a stand that their patrons are going to identify with.

Barbara: I like the discover line too—a little less authoritative

Kathy: i get the feeling that in-depth, process-oriented questions would be welcomed here . . .

Kathleen: they could convey that stand differently—"information you can trust," something like that

Susan: Discover could connect with users, authority connects with professionals

Nancy: it seems a little redundant to use both "authoritative" and "expert"

Barbara: i like the "what to expect"—the patron can take a peek before asking?

Kawanna: I like the fact that they promote the skills that librarians have—might increase the respect that we receive.

Emily: It's not catchy or friendly, but sets the library apart from Google Answers or other for-fee ask-a services . . .

Kathy: also [service name] suggests a relaxed atmosphere . . . not rushed . . .

Daria: Kathy, good statement. Does your tagline really say what you do or is it misleading?

Kathleen: But, authority sounds too much like, I'm talking and you're listening, 'cuz I'm the expert here

Linda: but we do want to be thought of as experts

Karen: yes, maybe they should emphasize the conversation aspect of cafe

Kathleen: Yes, but we don't want to be thought of as "snobby" experts, do we?

Kathy: i think they convey that quite well . . . i really like this site

Linda: no not snobby but authoritative

Kathleen: I barely noticed the "powered by your library" line underneath, but now I see it I really like it

Susan: I guess this comes back to how we view our role and how we want to be perceived

Emily: I think the potential for 'snobby' is offset by the pastel colors and overall mood of the logo.

Karen: what sort of expectations do we build into the tag/presentation?

Kathleen: Emily, I agree, for this site. But if they're using the tagline elsewhere, like on bus advertisements or radio ads, you may not get the rest of the visual message you're getting here.

Kathleen: Daria, how *did* the service market itself?

Karen: [Web page sent: explanation of scope of VR service] oops, sorry I didn't mean to send another page . . .

Kathleen: But I'm glad you did—I wanted to see this one!

Daria: Beyond the website, using brochures, news releases, flyers. Some of the typical promotions. But it was the name that really got peoples' interest.

Linda: if marketing requires knowing your audience, how do you market to an audience that is very diverse in education & background?

Kathleen: I think you have to use different marketing campaigns to target those diverse segments

Barbara: start with your regular library users

Karen: internet cafe is a well known term

Susan: Where do they get their information? Go there

Barbara: then hit the public with a huge blitz for a special time—

Barbara: library week?

Karen: yes, going to where THEY are

Emily: Perhaps they're already starting with a particular segment for this service . . . folks who use computers off-site.

Kathleen: Yes, it certainly looks that way.

Kathy: you do the ad campaign that will give the most bang for the buck

Karen: there was mention of instruction in schools, promoting the service in the classroom

Susan: Yes sometimes you limit yourself to a small target audience first and move up

Nancy: That's why it's important to have defined target audiences, just as Susan says

Nancy: you can't reach everyone all at once—the messages would be different

Nancy: especially in a public library environment

Linda: we want to partner with high schools for VR service and high school students would be a good bet for using this service

Karen: if you start in the schools the kids will relay to parents perhaps

Kathleen: Ooohh . . . isn't that what's called "viral marketing"? Start with a group that will spread the word, like a virus?

Linda: build a ball park and they will come

Daria: Let's take a look at some service descriptions, another element of branding [slide sent: pictures of four virtual reference service logos]

Karen: now, if we could make it SMELL good

Kathy: scratch, sniff and ask?

Kathleen: Karen, LOL!! I'm sure the technology is coming.

Emily: Scratch & Sniff Virtual Cafe!

Daria: This is the [University] website. [Web page sent: University Virtual Reference Service]

Barbara: i like the electric mouse the best

Daria: Look at the service description

Kawanna: Looks painful

Karen: religious connotations?

Kathleen: I don't like this logo! And they don't even get the semi-quote right: in Frankenstein, it was "it's alive!"

Kawanna: Makes it sound like they don't do actual reference.

Nancy: well, i think they mean it to be a play on words, right?

Karen: is VR a monster

Daria: What is good about this page is they are up front about their service.

Kathy: yep—they need an audio clip with a Peter Lorre type voice saying "it's alive"

Barbara: from the sublime to the ridiculous, then? a combo of Michelangelo and Mary Shelley?

Kathleen: But I like the "Got a Question?" line, and the service description acknowledges that confusion is normal and librarians are just waiting to help

Susan: Very simple. Clear and understandable I think the patron would know what the service is

Nancy: So we truly are confused—as they say! I like the idea of an audio! that would really catch the attention of users!

Barbara: the browser info is not snobby but allows the user to be referred elsewhere for help

Linda: i think the image will stay with patrons

Kathleen: The good thing about this (ugly) logo is that it appears on each page of the library's website, in the left-hand button bar. And because it's so ugly and jarring, it really stands out!

Linda: having it on each page is definitely a plus

Nancy: so it eventually would have branding recognition for their students

Susan: I like the Got a Question? part best, not It's live

Kathleen: The "TM" notice is interesting, too. Libraries are moving into trademarking their names—which means we'll have to be careful about "borrowing" service names from other places

Karen: the red bolts are eyecatching

Kawanna: It probably had immediate branding recognition for students.

Susan: If they didn't follow with the tagline—got a question—patrons may not realize what this is for

Nancy: good point about trademarking—libraries are notorious for adopting/adapting ideas from other libraries! share and share alike!

Karen: the interesting thing is clicking on the logo or Got A Question take you to the same place i think

Kathleen: Right, Nancy. And if too many entities "borrow" your name, you lose the inherent trademark. I don't think this is a bad thing, in the context of libraries . . . but we'll have to be aware of it

Susan: Maybe they couldn't make up their minds or had two strong ideas and couldn't choose

Barbara: flip side of copyright watchdogs . . .

Karen: two strong ideas, two ways of finding things . . . visual and literal

Emily: Now they just need an annoying jingle that gets stuck in your head . . .

Nancy: Karen, I hadn't thought of it that way!

Linda: jingles work great—someone could market them to libraries

Kathleen: Oooh, annoying jingle! That plays when you click on the logo! or that gets piped into the library stacks

Nancy: Now that sounds like a fun job—writing jingles!

Karen: stop the bubble machine!

Barbara: call Barry Manilow now!

Linda: stop the wrong answer machine

Nancy: the jingle could differ depending on audience!

Daria: [Public Library System] website. [Web page sent: County Public Library home page]

Susan: I like the idea of universal library branding—Patrons would really "know' what to expect anyway

Kathleen: Susan, I think this is what ALA was after with their "@ your library" campaign

Daria: [Web page sent: County Public Library links and information for e-mail, live chat, and phone reference service] We have ask a librarian. Then a different [service name]. Which one is it? Do we have an identity crisis?

Linda: I like that ask a librarian is explained

Karen: odd logo

Susan: We are competing with real big boys out there for patrons' time

Kathleen: I thought this library did a pretty good job of catching the eye and providing explanatory info. And they promise answers in 20 minutes. But the actual service was disappointing

Kawanna: I like that they refer those with questions related to circulation (i.e. hold) to the correct numbers to call.

Barbara: clear in the center—looks like logo is cut off at top

Daria: how about the tag line?

Kawanna: logo is a little busy

Barbara: like the basic info. links

Karen: I like Welcome

Karen: don't see welcome very often online

Nancy: i don't see the tagline on this screen—or do you mean "our live chat service"

Linda: when you need to know is good

Susan: Statement of service?

Kathy: kind of sounds like "stop by and chat . . . about anything."

Daria: any wording under your logo is considered a tag line.

Kathleen: It's weird—on their home page, it's a little green logo with "Ask a Librarian" and the line "Have a question. . . . Ask a librarian." I like that better.

Nancy: mixed taglines, then

Karen: perhaps [second service name] is the chat portion. i think it shows various ways of asking. is this image meant to be the person being asked?

Kathy: which is good for people not familiar with chat . . .

Nancy: This is their new marketing campaign!

Daria: I think this page refers to all services and [second service name] is just chat.

Nancy: they have bookmarks and notepads with this design/logo [web page image of perplexed man looking at alligator emerging from toilet while typing question on computer keyboard]

Emily: Variety of modes is nice, but I'm confused. What about branding consistency?

Daria: I don't understand the image.

Kawanna: Very interesting visual choice

Susan: I like "ask a librarian" better than "chat" which sounds too vague for the service offered and we use it!

Karen: i think it's good to see the options right up front. all three modes are asking a librarian

Daria: Emily is right. I sense confusion.

Barbara: he needs advice as to what to do

Kawanna: I think it is referring to an old urban legend . . .

Kathleen: I don't get it either. And even I wouldn't be wasting time asking a librarian with that kind of problem in the house.

Nancy: "chat," though, is certainly understood very readily by those who use it regularly—especially kids, but others too

Karen: loo-king for answers

Daria: Karen, that is stretching!

Kawanna: Just trying to make sense of a "very" odd picture . . .

Linda: he's every kid so they are targeting young adult males

Kathleen: Maybe the alligator needs to ask a librarian how to deal with this unfriendly human? The next step in the marketing campaign would have the alligator at the keyboard . . .

Daria: Let's look at one more library before we close out. Another University website. [Web page sent: University Virtual Reference Service with image of student seated at computer]

Daria: Any thoughts? Service description clear?

Barbara: the student looks tired

Kawanna: Is it strange that they actually show us "our" current time?

Barbara: clear

Karen: discussion space is interesting, emphasizes the conversation aspect of reference

Kathleen: This is actually kind of cute—bright, reassuring, and yet the "any time of the night" concept comes through

Barbara: good explanation of what times, schedule and holidays

Kathy: but they're not open at night . . .

Emily: Dude looks tired . . . working late at night, but their discussion space is only open until 5pm.

Daria: what about the logo?

Kawanna: Especially if their hours are 9 to 5 (I'm assuming this is their local time).

Linda: i went here early and found the time for west coast unhelpful in determining if their service was up

Daria: Is there a disconnect?

Barbara: AHA! Problem here . . .

Kathleen: Good point, Emily—the picture is clearly conveying something that contradicts the text

Kawanna: looks like a prescription logo.

Barbara: logo is dull

Kathy: i'm assuming they're on "summer hours" already

Barbara: looks like all the express transport services

Susan: why would they change from the initial web page real help right now to rx express? the first is good to keep!

Daria: Lets not forget the audience. who are your potential users? [Slide sent: Who are your potential users? Which group will you target for your marketing efforts?]

Karen: I like the viral approach

Susan: Students

Susan: and faculty!

Karen: schools

Kathy: yeah, but some of us old folks are immune to viruses.

Barbara: we can't do that here—we have to teach IL to our classes and VR will certainly be included

Daria: Just some questions to take away with you.

Kawanna: Tough questions—some of the libraries offer services to a larger audience, so their marketing is going to be vastly different from those who require users to have library cards, etc.

Daria: one last slide. How will you know you are ready for marketing?

Barbara: policy will dictate who uses the service

Susan: If we want to justify the costs of VR we also have to show we tried to find an audience

Daria: You need a clear scope of service, memorable name and graphics, tagline and need to know your potential users.

Kathy: that implies pre-testing logo, name. etc

Kawanna: I think a few of the services may have skipped a few steps . . .

Karen: that seems to be the crux—presenting it and then marketing? trying it out and then marketing?

Daria: It implies much pre-work before implementing a marketing plan

Barbara: once you start this you can't change for a while

Barbara: so it had better be right the first time

Nancy: yes, but even if you don't skip them, it's a huge challenge!

Barbara: which means good thinking first

Susan: Really means pre-planning before you jump in

Linda: we often skimp on the pre-work

Nancy: If you spend a lot of time doing these things, you might never get your service off the ground!!

Barbara: plan, plan, plan

Kathy: plan to be flexible tho

Daria: I know some of you have to go. Thanks for participating

Kathy: gotta go do desk . . . bye.

Kawanna: Bye everyone.

Linda: thanks for this class—it was great, bye

Nancy: Thanks for another great meeting—I'm going to miss all of you!

Karen: yes, thank you for this class!

Nancy: We need to keep in touch—let's do Yahoo with our own names—gasp!!

Susan: This has been a great class. Now if only powers that be want input . . .

APPENDIX

Other Support Materials

TRAINER ORIENTATION AGENDA CHEAT SHEETS

The following information was printed in Arial Bold, font size fourteen to sixteen, on a separate page for each orientation activity. Trainers placed the sheets next to the keyboard, using the notes as a guide to the day's progress and a reminder of procedures and facts. A line separates the information that was printed on each page.

9:00 to 9:45 AM

Introductions

Walking Billboards

Handout in binder (1 page)

9:45 to 10:30 AM

AGENDA FOR ORIENTATION in binder

Introduce web pages:
readings, activities, assignments
Overview of training curriculum
(PowerPoint slides)

http://wlo.statelib.wa.gov/services/vrs/VRSTrain/first.cfm (This should be set as the home page for each PC when we arrive the day of orientation.)
PowerPoint overview of the Anytime, Anywhere Answers training curriculum, the methods of delivery, and expectations for learners and trainers. (Download free viewer if you do not have PowerPoint on your computer.)

For a full-screen view of the PowerPoint slides, right click on the first slide and select Full Screen.

Syllabus—is linked to Trainer Tips only—save in Word before class starts.

add dates to syllabus (especially important to set a time for our virtual meetings)
discuss times and dates for online meetings
Print syllabus—distribute

10:45 to 11:15 AM

CORE COMPETENCIES FOR VIRTUAL REFERENCE

handout in binder

Learners complete Initial Skills Assessment (note three-month follow-up)

handout in binder
collect and send to Project Coordinator

11:15 AM to Noon

VIRTUAL REFERENCE: A WORK IN PROGRESS (POWERPOINT SLIDES)

A look at the history, current status, and future of virtual reference services in libraries

handout in binder

Link from First Week web page

Show the PowerPoint slides on Virtual Reference: A Work in Progress

Use the link for the presentation slides, but use the PDF file as your presentation notes

5-page printout in trainer notebook (before training, go through this printout and mark the text that accompanies each slide)

1:30 to 2:15 PM

Taking the First Steps to Training

Identity-neutral e-mail account

fastmail.fm

Registering for AIM Express and setting up buddy list

http://www.aim.com/get_aim/express/aim_expr.adp

Discussion lists

Ask the learners to sign up for the two electronic discussion lists (DIG_REF and VRSTRAINA or VRSTRAINB) when they are back at work, using their work e-mail accounts. You will need to tell them which of the VRSTRAIN lists to subscribe to.

2:15 to 2:45 PM

ANSWERING QUESTIONS USING CHAT

2-page PDF in binder—easiest to look at questions here

Link from First Week web page

This is a half-hour session

Get everyone to AIM page

linked from previous session

once signed in, should have the Buddy List box open, >>add partner's name using =?-setup

Pair people up with someone they are not sitting next to, give them about 10 minutes' practice, then have them switch roles.

2:45 to 3:15 PM

TIPS FOR SUCCESS WITH ONLINE LEARNING

Learner expectations

Go over the Tips for Success with Online Learning, stressing how important it will be for the learners to communicate their time expectations to their supervisors and coworkers, and to complete assignments on time. We expect the learners to do their training activities on work time, using library computers.

LEARNER SUPPORT NEEDED

Hardware and software requirements

This training curriculum works best with Windows 2000, Internet Explorer 5 or 6, with the latest version of Acrobat Reader installed. If PowerPoint is not installed on their computers, they can download the free PowerPoint viewer from Microsoft. The training designers are aware of the problems in using Acrobat Reader with Windows XP and will suggest some fixes for those who have to use XP.

3:30 to 4:15 PM

A look at the 24/7 Reference software and some practice using its online meeting functions.

From First Week web page

Norms for Online Meetings—PDF, GO OVER THESE NORMS!

http://ref3.247ref.org (set up in Favorites on each PC prior to start of class)

Clear cache

Use the meeting key provided by the trainers

Username XXXX

Password XXXX

Meeting key

For best results, change screen resolution to approximately 1025×750. Start>Settings>Control>Panel>Display>Settings.

Use bright yellow handout in trainer notebook

Practice with the 24/7 online meeting software

Topics for online meetings:

Week 2: no topic—discuss Virtual Field Trips or readings

Week 3: Information Literacy and Virtual Reference

Week 4: Service Evaluation and Continuous Improvement

Week 5: Marketing Virtual Reference

4:15 to 4:45 PM

SELF-ASSESSMENT OF WINDOWS MULTITASKING SKILLS AND INTERNET REFERENCE SKILLS

Assessments

These two self-assessments (Windows Multitasking and Internet Reference Competencies) should be completed by learners but not turned in. The first was mailed and learners should bring completed copies to class. These can be used to identify areas for improvement. (A "Sort of" equals NO!) Less than 75 percent proficiency on either assessment means that the learners should consider ways to upgrade their skills.

How to upgrade these skills

For the Internet Reference Competencies, there are two excellent self-paced courses. Joe Barker at the University of California at Berkeley provides a tutorial on web-searching skills, which is updated regularly. Debbie Flanagan's tutorial on search strategies has practice exercises.

If they need some help with multitasking skills and Windows Desktop control, there is a self-paced exercise provided (Keys to Organizing Your Virtual Reference Desk).

PRACTICE EXERCISE: Instructions and Questions for Paired Chat during Orientation

Instructions

During this exercise, you will be chatting with [Screen Name]. Sign on to instant messaging and send a chat invitation to your partner. Decide who will ask a question (patron) and who will answer (librarian).

If you are the patron with a question:

- Select one of the questions below or make up your own.
- You may decide to play the role of a student with a homework assignment, a person with a trivia question, etc.
- Word your question and responses accordingly.
- When the librarian sends a URL to you, open a second browser window [CTRL N]. (You can use CTRL C and CTRL V to copy and paste the URL into the second browser window.)
- Let the librarian know if this website answers your question.

If you are the librarian answering the question:

- Clarify the patron's question through a reference interview.
- Open a second browser window [CTRL N] and search for websites that will answer the question.
- Once you find a good source for the answer, use CTRL C and CTRL V to copy and paste the URL in the chat window.
- Keep the patron informed about what you are doing.

- Check to see if the patron is satisfied with what you found.
- Then trade roles.

Practice Questions

1. I would like to know the specific death dates of Jessie and Frank James. Where did they die?
2. When did Mount St. Helens erupt?
3. What is the date for Ramadan in 2004?
4. I am writing an essay on teenage suicide. I am looking for sources of teenagers giving personal testimonies who have decided not to commit suicide or have tried suicide and lived.
5. When is Juneteenth celebrated?
6. Who was the first person to walk on the moon?
7. Why do potatoes turn green beneath the skin?
8. I am looking for a playdough recipe.
9. What is the history behind the Nobel prizes? When was the first one awarded?
10. When and where was the first World's Fair?
11. I need to know which states were the original thirteen colonies.
12. Who are the Chicago Seven defendants and what did they do?
13. What are the names of the nine muses?
14. Where do I find APA or MLA formats for bibliographies or works cited online?
15. What are the dates of the Black Monday and Black Thursday Stock Market Crashes?
16. When is Deaf Awareness Week?

GETTING CHATTY: Conversation at the Virtual Reference Desk

Library staff providing virtual reference frequently assume that their twelve- to seventeen-year-old users are the real chat fanatics, using instant messaging (IM) software to keep in touch with friends, do homework, ask someone out on a date, or share MP3s. It is true that this age group represents the largest percentage of chat usage (74 percent of online teens have used IM). But the increasing popularity of real-time text messaging is reaching all segments of the online population. IM has revolutionized the way companies do business and may be rewriting the rules of human conversation. It has been called the "e e cummings approach" to communication!

Some statistics from the Pew Internet and American Life Project report (June 2001):[1]

- 150 million people are IM users
- 1.3 billion messages are sent daily via AOL
- 44 percent of online American adults have used IM
- 4.9 billion minutes were spent on work-related IM in September 2001

Deciphering the Code

For those who frequently use IM, a shorthand language has evolved. Here's an example:

JASON:	hey sup
Way2Go:	nm, u?
JASON:	nm just chillin
Way2Go:	do you have lotta work?
JASON:	mad amount of english, u?
Way2Go:	english 2
JASON:	brb
JASON:	back
Way2Go:	k
JASON:	did you checkout that site?
Way2Go:	um, no?
JASON:	my gf told me about it
JASON:	kool…iykwim
JASON:	alright g2g pos
Way2Go:	bye
JASON:	ttyl bye

What did these two people say to each other? Probably nm!

Chat Translator

Here is some of the shorthand commonly used in IM conversations. Anything in all uppercase is considered shouting, or a more adamant or urgent expression.

afaik =	As far as I know
brb =	Be right back
btw =	By the way
def =	Definitely
fav =	Favorite
g2g =	Got to go
h/w =	Homework
idk =	I don't know
imho =	In my humble opinion
iykwim =	If you know what I mean
j/k =	Just kidding
k =	Okay
lol =	Laughing out loud
lp or /last =	Last post
lpfn =	Last post for now
more =	The message you are reading is only part of a thought and more is coming.
ne1 =	Anyone
nm =	Not much, nothing much
pos =	Parent over shoulder
rotfl =	Rolling on the floor, laughing
sh =	Same here
smthg =	Something
sn =	Screen name
tia =	Thanks in advance
ttyl =	Talk to you later
UK? =	Are you okay?
ur =	You are
y =	Why

"Chat 101" provides glossaries of chat acronyms, abbreviations, emoticons, and terms.[2]

Chatting at the Virtual Reference Desk

Depending on your users, you may or may not encounter "chat lingo" in your virtual reference transactions. Here are some tips for an effective reference transaction using chat. Remember that there are no auditory or visual cues to indicate emotion or reaction!

Be welcoming and personable. Use the patron's name if appropriate. Reply to his/her specific question, using scripted responses thoughtfully. Type like you would talk. You can match the conversational tone of your patron's posts without using slang, shorthand, or emoticons. Don't use library jargon or abbreviations.

It's OK to use short phrases and informal language . . . don't get hung up on grammar and punctuation!!! . . . use three or four periods between words to indicate pauses. Break up long responses into shorter blocks (two or three sentences). Type the first part, make your last word "more," and continue the message in your next post. Avoid the Caps Lock key. Typing in all capitals is considered yelling.

Be as clear and concise as possible without being abrupt. Be careful to word your messages in a way that communicates helpfulness ("Were you able to check in our online catalog?" *not* "You already checked the online catalog, right?")

Keep the conversation flowing. Thirty seconds of dead air is a long time for the patron. Try to establish a rhythm of sending a message every 30 to 45 seconds or less. ("I am going to check some printed sources." "I am still searching.")

Let the patron know what you are doing. ("I'm sending you a web page now.")

Allow enough time for the patron to read, think, and respond before your next posting. Ask for cues from the patron about pacing. ("Let me know when you see the page that I sent." "Let me know when you are ready . . . ")

If the question will take more time to answer, keep the patron informed and give him/her something to do in the meantime. ("While I am checking, you may want to look at this web page.")

In chat reference, users are more anonymous, which may reduce inhibitions. You don't have to tolerate abusive or offensive language, but don't take impatience or abruptness personally. The Pew Report reveals that *37 percent of teens using IM* have written something that they would not have said face-to-face.

Want to Read More about Chat and IM?

"Instant Messaging Phenom Is, Like, Way beyond E-Mail," *U.S. News and World Report*, March 5, 2001, 54–56.[3]

KEYS TO ORGANIZING YOUR VIRTUAL REFERENCE DESK

First Step: Organize Your Desktop

DESKTOP REAL ESTATE

Have you heard the term "desktop real estate"? Basically it means how much stuff can fit on your computer screen. It is directly related to your display resolution—the maximum number of pixels that can be displayed on a monitor.

This number is always expressed as some number of horizontal pixels times some number of vertical pixels. Common display resolution settings include 800×600, 1024×768, 1162×864, and 1280×1024. As display resolution increases, desktop real estate increases. More real estate means that everything on the screen—icons, fonts, menus, and buttons—shrinks in size.

If you would like to change your monitor's resolution to get more desktop real estate, follow these directions:

1. Go to your Desktop, right-click anywhere, and choose Properties to launch the Display Properties.
2. Click the Settings tab.
3. Under "Screen area," move the slider to the right to increase your resolution. As you do this, the simulated display shrinks everything on-screen.
4. Try setting your screen area to 1024×768.
5. Click Apply.
6. You will be greeted with a pop-up window that says your screen may flicker during the resizing process. Click OK.
7. If you do not like your new resolution setting, click Cancel and try again. Click OK if everything looks good.

After adjusting your monitor resolution, you may need to tweak the monitor's settings to resize its horizontal and vertical positions.

QUICK LAUNCH

For frequently used applications, simply drag a desktop icon to the Quick Launch portion of the Windows Taskbar (this is the area to the immediate right of the Start menu). Clicking on any Quick Launch icon allows you to start a program, such as Internet Explorer, without going to the desktop. (This is the best way to open a second browser window while you are helping a patron in the Librarian Console.)

ACCESSING MY COMPUTER

If you need fast access to My Computer, drag the My Computer icon from the Desktop to the Start button. Now you have created a cascading shortcut to all the My Computer functionality, which expands to reveal all your drives, folders, and files.

Second Step: Learn Multitasking and Keyboard Shortcuts

When you are helping patrons in co-browsing or materials-sharing sessions, you may have as many as five windows open at once. Here are some tips and tricks to help you manage multiple windows successfully.

Keep track of the windows that you have opened by looking at the Taskbar. You can cycle through each window by holding down the ALT key, then pressing down the TAB key. Release both keys to view the selected window. Each window has Minimize, Restore, and Close buttons in the upper right corner. You can also right-click anywhere on the blue title bar to get a menu for the same functions.

WINDOWS LOGO KEY

The fastest way to minimize a number of open windows, or to go to the Desktop, is to use the Windows logo key (located on the keyboard between the CTRL and ALT keys). Here are some useful Windows logo key commands:

Windows logo:	Opens the Start menu
Windows logo + M:	Minimize all open windows
SHIFT + Windows logo + M:	Undo minimize all
Windows logo + D:	Goes to the Desktop (This acts as a toggle. Use it again to return to your previously open window.)
Windows logo + E:	Opens Windows Explorer

KEYBOARD COMMANDS

Here are the most commonly used keyboard commands that work in any Windows application:

CTRL + A:	Select all
CTRL + C:	Copy
CTRL + X:	Cut
CTRL + V:	Paste
CTRL + Z:	Undo the last command
CTRL + Y:	Repeat the last command
CTRL + F:	Find a word in this document or on this web page

Hint: If you forget these keyboard commands, you can always see them in the pull-down File and Edit menus for any Windows application.

RIGHT MOUSE BUTTON

All Windows operating systems since Windows 98 make extensive use of the right mouse button. You can right-click anything on the Desktop, including the Taskbar. Right-clicking on the Taskbar allows you to cascade or minimize all open windows. Our advice is to right-click anything and everything just to see what happens! The keyboard equivalent of the right mouse button is SHIFT + F10.

HIGHLIGHTING ITEMS IN DROP-DOWN MENUS

To select or highlight two or more items in a drop-down menu, hold down the SHIFT key for consecutive items, the CTRL key for non-consecutive items.

USING WINDOWS EXPLORER

Windows Explorer is your hierarchical cabinet for all the folders and files on your computer and on your network. You can use Windows Explorer to move, copy, rename, view, save, and delete files and folders. Unfortunately, Microsoft considers Windows Explorer an expert's tool and makes it difficult to find. Your best method of opening Windows Explorer is to use Windows logo + E. Another way is to right-click the Start menu and select Explore.

Third Step: Practice Browser Tips and Tricks

In Internet Explorer, you can store and organize frequently used web links using the Favorites menu or the Links toolbar. Using the Links toolbar is quick and easy because you can drag the icon from the Address bar directly to the Links toolbar. Or drag any link from a web page onto the Links toolbar. Once you have a set of links there, you can use the right mouse button to move, rename, delete, etc.

You can place folders on the Links toolbar with these steps:

1. Go to the Favorites menu.
2. Click Organize Favorites.
3. Click on the Links folder.
4. Click on the Create Folder button.
5. Drag and drop your links into the new folder.

SAVE A FILE TO SHARE

When you want to share a file that you have found on a web page (e.g., PDF files such as tax forms), follow these simple steps to save the file:

1. Right click on the link to the file (do not open the file).
2. Choose "Save target as."
3. Change the location to save the file to your desktop. From there it is easy to use the Materials Sharing function of your virtual reference software.

CLEARING CACHE

Your browser stores graphics and text from the websites you visit. This information is stored in files on your hard drive called "cache" or Temporary Internet Files. It is quicker for the browser to pull graphics and text from the cache than downloading the entire site again. Unfortunately, over time, your browser's cache grows. A cache full of outdated information is worse than no cache at all. It causes problems with Java applets, causes you to see out-of-date text or images, and makes your browser sluggish. Also, with the virtual reference software developed by 24/7 and LSSI, you must clear the cache before you begin any monitoring session.

Here's how to clear cache and Temporary Internet Files.

Netscape 4.X

- Select Edit, and then click on Preferences.
- Select Advanced, and then click Cache.
- Click on Clear Memory Cache and Clear Disk Cache buttons.

Explorer 5.X or 6.X

- Select Tools, then click on Internet Options.
- Select the General tab.
- Click on Delete Files.

AOL

- Select My AOL.
- Select Preferences, and then click WWW.
- Select Delete Files.

KEYBOARD SHORTCUTS

You can use keyboard shortcuts to perform common browser functions (in both Netscape and Internet Explorer) and give your mouse hand a break.

Home:	Jumps to beginning of page
End:	Jumps to end of page
Esc:	Stops loading current page
F5:	Refreshes the screen
F11:	Toggles between full screen and regular view of the browser window. (Good for screenshots.)
Back Space:	Goes back one page
Alt + Left Arrow:	Goes back to the previous page
Alt + Right Arrow:	Goes forward to the next page
Alt + Home:	Goes to your home page
Ctrl + N:	Opens a new browser window. (Be careful with this method of opening a new browser window. The new window will be identical to the one that is active, so you might think that a new one wasn't really opened.)
Ctrl + R:	Reloads the current page
Ctrl + B:	Opens the Organize Favorites or Bookmarks window
Ctrl + D:	Adds the current web page to your Favorites or Bookmarks
Ctrl + H:	Opens the History folder
Ctrl + F:	Finds text on current page. (Remember that this works in Word Documents, Excel Spreadsheets, and more.)

OPENING A FRAME IN A NEW WINDOW

Navigating websites that use frames can be confusing, especially if you would like to send a link to someone or bookmark a page from a framed site. Both Internet Explorer and Netscape Navigator allow users to open a framed page in a new window. Right-click the link you want to open and choose Open Link in New Window from the menu. The frame will appear in its own browser window. Remember that this does not work in the 24/7 Reference or LSSI Librarian Consoles.

HIGHLIGHTING THE COMPLETE URL

Sometimes the URL displayed in the address bar is very long. To highlight the complete URL, click three times in the address bar, then use CTRL C to copy or CTRL V to paste.

INSTALLING AND USING ACROBAT READER

To view and print PDF (Portable Document Format) files requires Acrobat Reader software. Many people successfully download the free software but then don't know how to install it. It helps your patrons if you have some clear, step-by-step instructions (see http://whyfiles.larc.nasa.gov/text/educators/help/tutorials/download_acrobat.html) for downloading and installing Acrobat Reader. With PDF files, you use the Acrobat Reader toolbar for various functions, including Print, Find on Page, Select Text or Graphic, Copy, etc.

Fourth Step: Make Your Web Searching Efficient and Effective

INSTALL THE GOOGLE TOOLBAR

If Google is your search engine of first choice, install the Google Toolbar (http://toolbar.google.com) in your browser. Using this toolbar, you can enter your search terms from the browser toolbar itself, without going to the Google start page. You also have one-click access to Google Image searching or to the advanced search screen. Use the highlight function of the Google Toolbar to find your search terms on the web page. *Important note:* If you have already installed the Google Toolbar, check which version you are using. There was a security flaw in the early versions. If you have any version prior to 1.1.59, uninstall it and reinstall the newest version.

DUAL WINDOW BROWSING

Here's a nifty trick to use with a page of search engine results. You can drag links from one window to another for faster surfing. Instead of clicking on a link and waiting for the page to load, you can speed up your searching by using more than one browser window. Open two browser windows next to each other (or cascade them). Then simply drag a link from the page you are reading and drop it into the other window. To do this, left-click the link and drag it to the other browser window, then release the mouse button. The link will automatically load into the window.

TIPS FOR SUPER SEARCHERS

Here are some tips for maximizing your web searching:

1. Choose the right tool for the question. Don't use a search engine when a directory will give you better, more authoritative results.
2. Take a few seconds to think through the search terms that you will use.
3. Use a concept search engine like Teoma (http://www.teoma.com) to gather related terms.
4. Learn to quickly use the advanced search features in Google.
5. Know how to find the information contained in databases that are "invisible" to search engines.[4]
6. Use "wedge words." These are words to use in your search query to find specific types of documents. Examples are "FAQ," "comparison chart," and "database."[5]
7. Subscribe to regular e-mail reports on search engines (Search Day or Search Engine Watch).[6]
8. Organize the sites that you use most frequently, using the Links toolbar, Favorites, your own web page, or web-based bookmarks.
9. If your search strategy clearly isn't working, try something else!

NOTES

1. Pew Internet and American Life Project, "Teenage Life Online: The Rise of the Instant-Message Generation and the Internet's Impact on Friendships and Family Relationships," June 20, 2001, http://pewinternet.org/reports/toc.asp?Report=36. See also "The Digital Disconnect: The Widening Gap between Internet-Savvy Students and Their Schools," August 14, 2002, http://pewinternet.org/reports/toc.asp?Report=67. More recent information is in "The Ever-Shifting Internet Population: A New Look at Internet Access and the Digital Divide," April 16, 2003, http://pewinternet.org/reports/toc.asp?Report=88.
2. "Chat 101" is available at http://www.ker95.com/chat101/html/chatterms.html.
3. "Instant Messaging Phenom" is available at http://www.usnews.com/usnews/nycu/tech/articles/010305/nycu/im.htm.
4. "Invisible Web" search tips are available at http://home.earthlink.net/~rosskenw/search.html.
5. "Wedge word" tips are available at http://marylaine.com/exlibris/xlib94.html.
6. Information on search engines is available at http://www.searchenginewatch.com.

APPENDIX H

Anytime, Anywhere Answers Budget, March 2002–June 2003

C urriculum Development Contract	$21,000
24/7 Reference Software License	5,000
Desktop Publishing Software License	500
Trainer Fees (eight classes, two trainers assigned to each)	16,000
Travel	1,000
Washington State Library's Staff Time	20,000
Course Materials (binders, printing)	300
Miscellaneous (orientation refreshments, office supplies, etc.)	250
TOTAL	$64,050

APPENDIX

I Trainer Notes and Tips

ABOUT THIS APPROACH TO TRAINING

This training curriculum is based on a constructivist approach to distance learning. Some characteristics of constructivism are:

stresses collaboration over individual learning
more learner-focused, less teacher-focused
contextual, builds on previous learner experiences
emphasizes exploration, discovery, and reflection

As a trainer, your most important roles will be to:

support and encourage the learners, providing extra assistance whenever needed
facilitate an active, collaborative learning environment
provide positive feedback on each learner's contributions
ask the right question rather than give the right answer

Preparation

Using the syllabus, fill in the specific dates for all of the training activities and assignments. Print out copies of the completed syllabus and distribute them to the learners at the face-to-face orientation. Also print out the Learner List to record the e-mail addresses and screen names that your learners will be using during the five weeks of training.

There is also a Learner Completion Checklist that can be used to keep track of those who attended online meetings and when assignments are completed.

Face-to-Face Orientation and First Week

Here is an agenda [linked file] for the orientation, with times allotted to each of the activities. All PowerPoint, PDF, and Word files can be downloaded, viewed, or printed directly from the training web pages. For a full-screen view of the PowerPoint slides, right-click on the first slide and select Full Screen. Pass out copies of the syllabus at the conclusion of the PowerPoint overview. Show the PowerPoint slides on Virtual Reference: A Work in Progress, using the PDF file as your presentation notes.

SECRET PATRON DISCUSSION

In previous classes, some learners have expressed discomfort with the Secret Patron activity. Use the sample Secret Patron scenario and transcript to illustrate the value of the exercise.

ONLINE DISCUSSION LISTS

Ask the learners to sign up for the two lists (DIG_REF and VRSTRAIN) when they are back at work, using their work e-mail accounts. You will need to tell them which of the VRSTRAIN lists to subscribe to—either VRSTRAINA or VRSTRAINB.

LEARNER EXPECTATIONS

Go over the Tips for Success with Online Learning, stressing how important it will be for the learners to communicate their time expectations to their supervisors and coworkers, and to complete assignments on time. We expect the learners to do their training activities on work time, using library computers.

HARDWARE AND SOFTWARE REQUIREMENTS

This training curriculum works best with Windows 2000 and Internet Explorer 5 or 6, with the latest version of Acrobat Reader installed. If PowerPoint is not installed on learners' computers, they can download the free PowerPoint viewer from Microsoft. The training designers are aware of the problems in using Acrobat Reader with Windows XP and will suggest some fixes for those who have to use XP.

ASSESSMENTS

Distribute printed copies of the Initial Skills Assessment of Competencies for Virtual Reference and have the learners fill them out. Collect them after completion. Mail these assessments to Buff Hirko at the Washington State Library.

There are two other self-assessments (Windows Multitasking and Internet Reference Competencies) that the learners can complete but don't have to turn in. These can be used to identify areas for improvement. (A "Sort of" equals No!) Less than 75 percent proficiency on either assessment means that the learners should consider ways to upgrade their skills.

For the Internet Reference Competencies, there are two excellent self-paced courses. Joe Barker at the University of California at Berkeley provides a tutorial (http://www.lib.berkeley.edu/TeachingLib/Guides/Internet/Findinfo.html) on web-searching skills, which is updated regularly. Debbie Flanagan's tutorial (http://home.sprintmail.com/~debflanagan/main.html) on search strategies has practice exercises.

If learners need some help with multitasking skills and Windows Desktop control, there is a self-paced exercise provided (Keys to Organizing Your Virtual Reference Desk).

ENDING THE FIRST DAY ORIENTATION

A good way to end the day is with a reminder of what the learners need to do when they return to work (e.g., sign up for discussion lists, put online meeting dates on their calendars, verify their time commitments with supervisors, etc.). Have them generate the list and write it on a whiteboard or pad of paper.

ANNOUNCEMENT OF ONLINE MEETING

Before the end of the First Week, send out an announcement, via the discussion list, of the Second Week chat meeting. The announcement should include this information (copy and paste into the e-mail message):

> Date and Time of Chat Meeting ____________________
>
> Five minutes before the starting time for the meeting, go to AIM Express, http://www.aim.com/get_aim/express/aim_ expr.adp.
>
> Click on Start, then log in using your screen name and password.
>
> The trainers will send you an invitation to join a chat room.
>
> When you receive the invitation, click on the Go icon and enter the chat room.
>
> Remember to read the *Norms for Online Meetings.*

Ask the learners to reply to you so that you know they have successfully subscribed to the discussion list.

Second Week

Read the various postings to the discussion list on the Virtual Field Trips activity. Summarize them briefly and highlight the most thoughtful insights, remembering to provide positive feedback for each individual learner's contribution.

Initiate and facilitate the chat meeting using AIM Express. There is no formal topic for this week's meeting. The objectives are to give learners more opportunities to practice their chat skills and to gain comfort with the meeting norms in preparation for next week's more formal online meeting. You and the other trainer can brainstorm a list of open-ended questions to ask, focusing on the Virtual Field Trips. What did they learn that they want to remember in planning and developing their own library's virtual reference service?

ANNOUNCEMENT OF ONLINE MEETING

Before the end of the Second Week, send out an announcement, via the discussion list, of the Third Week online meeting. The announcement should include this information (copy and paste into the e-mail message):

> Date and Time of Online Meeting ____________________
>
> Five to ten minutes before start of meeting, go to the training web pages and click on the link to the log-in screen.
>
> Remember to change your screen resolution to 1068×762 before joining the meeting.
>
> The meeting key is . . . .
>
> The topic for this meeting will be Information Literacy in Virtual Reference.
>
> Remember to follow the *Norms for Online Meetings.*
>
> It's important to complete the background readings and activities in preparation for the meeting.

Third Week

To each individual learner, e-mail a PDF file with the scenario that he/she will use for the Secret Patron activity. Using the VRS Sites Grid, choose three virtual reference sites to assign to each learner. The scenarios will dictate whether to choose a public or academic library. Be careful not to assign more than one library using 24/7 Reference because you may get the same librarian answering for the consortium!

Here are the PDF files for the Secret Patron scenarios: [25 linked files].

Read the various postings to the discussion list on the Secret Patron activity. Summarize them briefly and highlight the most thoughtful insights, remembering to provide positive feedback for each individual learner's contribution.

SOME CONTEXT FOR THE "SECRET PATRON" ACTIVITY

The Secret Patron activity is based on a "secret shopper" approach used in customer service skills training. Transform, Inc., uses a secret patron approach for evaluating library reference services as part of its Effective Reference Performance training. The University of Maryland College of Information Studies is also doing VRS evaluation research using a secret patron approach (they call it "unobtrusive observer").

The Secret Patron activity focuses on the myriad ways that our users express their questions. The activity explores the effectiveness of the chat reference interview in clarifying the user's questions. We have observed that when librarians practice chat reference with each other, they are very polite and they ask questions in ways that make sense to themselves and to other librarians. Our users don't do this!

Occasionally, learners do not want to participate in this specific activity because of disagreement or discomfort with the approach. As a trainer, it is essential to respect and honor your learners as adults who can articulate their needs. If this concern is expressed, explore with your learner what he/she wants to do to experience the virtual reference transaction from the user's perspective, in a way that is comfortable. The goal, as stated above, is to explore the reference interview from the user's perspective.

ONLINE MEETINGS USING THE 24/7 REFERENCE SOFTWARE

Starting in the Third Week, you will initiate and facilitate three weekly online meetings, using the 24/7 Reference software. The topics are Information Literacy in Virtual Reference, Service Evaluation and Continuous Improvement, and Marketing of Virtual Reference Services.

To initiate the meeting on Information Literacy, one trainer will log in to 24/7 Reference on the librarian side. This trainer will control the content of the meeting, pushing slides and pre-scripted messages to the attendees. Here are complete directions [linked file] for delivering an online meeting using this software. The other trainer should log-in to the meeting as a participant, using the meeting key. He/she will control the discussion, encouraging the learners to brainstorm and share ideas on the questions posed, and pointing out how these ideas are related to the materials and activities in the training. This trainer will act as queue keeper as described in the Norms for Online Meetings. (Use of the ! and ? is optional, depending on the needs of your learners.)

ANNOUNCEMENT OF ONLINE MEETING

Before the end of the Third Week, send out an announcement, via the discussion list, of the Fourth Week online meeting. The announcement should include this information (copy and paste into e-mail message):

Date and Time of Online Meeting ____________________

Five to ten minutes before the start of the meeting, go to the training web pages and click on the link to the log-in screen.

Remember to change your screen resolution to 1068×762 before joining the meeting.

The meeting key is . . . .

The topic for this meeting will be Service Evaluation and Continuous Improvement.

Remember to follow the *Norms for Online Meetings.*

It's important to complete the background readings and activities in preparation for the meeting.

Fourth Week

Send the chat transcripts [linked PDF files] to the learners via the discussion list. You may choose to use the chat transcripts from their Secret Patron activities instead of these. Ask the learners to read and comment on the transcripts. They should keep in mind the RUSA guidelines and the behaviors that are effective in both face-to-face and telephone reference. Do these behaviors appear in the transcripts? The learners will summarize their impressions of the transcripts, using the questions to guide their summaries.

Read the various postings to the discussion list on the chat transcripts. Summarize them briefly and highlight the most thoughtful insights, remembering to provide positive feedback for each individual learner's contribution.

Initiate and facilitate the online meeting on Service Evaluation.

ANNOUNCEMENT OF ONLINE MEETING

Before the end of the Fourth Week, send out an announcement, via the discussion list, of the Fifth Week online meeting. The announcement should include this information (copy and paste into e-mail message):

Date and Time of Online Meeting ____________________

Five to ten minutes before the start of the meeting, go to the training web pages and click on the link to the log-in screen.

Remember to change your screen resolution to 1068×762 before joining the meeting.

The meeting key is . . . .

The topic for this meeting will be Marketing of Virtual Reference Services.

Remember to follow the *Norms for Online Meetings*.

It's important to complete the background readings and activities in preparation for the meeting.

Fifth Week

Read the various postings to the discussion list on the Policies and Procedures activity. Summarize them briefly and highlight the most thoughtful insights, remembering to provide positive feedback for each individual learner's contribution.

Initiate and facilitate the online meeting on Marketing.

Thank the learners for their participation and for their individual contributions to the training. Ask them to fill out and send in the evaluation form. In three months they will receive a follow-up assessment on skills learned and retained.

Encourage the learners to keep in touch with each other and to continue to share their experiences with virtual reference.

Congratulations! You and the learners have completed Anytime, Anywhere Answers. We look forward to your comments and suggestions for future classes.

GLOSSARY

application sharing, also called **remote control:** feature that enables full desktop sharing between library staff and patron, with mutual mouse and keyboard control.

authentication: the process of identifying an individual, usually based on a user name and password or identification number. In security systems, authentication is distinct from authorization, which is the process of giving individuals access to system objects based on their identity. Authentication merely ensures that the individual is who he or she claims to be, but says nothing about the access rights of the individual.

blog, short for **web log:** a web page that serves as a publicly accessible journal, usually based on a specific topic. Typically updated daily, blogs may have either a single or multiple contributors.

browser, short for **web browser:** a software application used to locate and display web pages. The two most popular browsers are Netscape Navigator and Microsoft Internet Explorer.

chat, also called **interactive chat** or **live chat:** a software application that allows real-time communication between two users via computer. Once a chat session is initiated, either user can enter text by typing on the keyboard and the entered text will appear on the other user's monitor.

co-browsing, also called **escorting:** a feature of interactive chat software that allows the patron to see everything the library staff member sees as they navigate through web pages.

digital reference, often used interchangeably with **virtual reference:** a library service that provides answers to customers' questions via electronic means, such as e-mail, web form, interactive chat, or application sharing.

discussion list: an online mailing list that automatically broadcasts e-mail to everyone on the list. The result is similar to a newsgroup, except that the messages are available only to individuals on the list.

download: *see* plug-in.

e-mail management: the ability to identify, transfer, and maintain questions and answers based on status (e.g., new, pending, forwarded, updated, completed, rejected).

escorting: *see* co-browsing

operator: a library staff member who is using an interactive chat application in response to a patron request.

plug-in, also called **download:** a software module that adds a specific feature or service to a larger system that requires the user to download an application to his/her computer for use.

push: the ability to send a URL or document to a patron, resulting in the page being displayed on the patron's computer screen.

queue: a software feature that prioritizes patrons waiting for service, usually in calling order.

remote control: *see* application sharing.

screen sharing: the ability of a library staff member to see the screen displayed on the patron's computer

script: any of various canned answers to common questions that are chosen from a drop-down list of terms or phrases in order to reduce typing time and speed chat sessions.

seat: a licensing/pricing arrangement—one seat equals one library staff member currently logged into the service (multiple patrons may be logged in).

transcript: a written record of a reference chat session, including all of the librarian's and patron's typed statements and URLs, which can be sent to the patron, retained for future reference, archived, or otherwise utilized.

virtual reference, often used interchangeably with **digital reference**: a library service that provides answers to customers' questions via interactive chat or application-sharing software.

VoIP, abbreviation of **Voice over Internet Protocol** or **Video over Internet Protocol**: hardware (microphones and cameras) and software that enable use of the Internet to transmit live voice and video images.

BIBLIOGRAPHY

The following list includes all readings assigned to learners who participated in the Anytime, Anywhere Answers training program between November 2002 and June 2003.

REQUIRED READINGS

Arnoldy, Ben. "Paying for Answers Online." *Christian Science Monitor,* July 22, 2002, 14.

Association of College and Research Libraries. "Introduction to Information Literacy." http://www.ala.org/acrl/il/intro/newil.html. A concise introduction to information literacy.

Barber, Peggy, and Linda Wallace. "10 Tips for Marketing Virtual Reference Services." http://www.ssdesign.com/librarypr/download/odds_and_ends/marketing_vp. Created by Library Communication Strategies and presented at the American Library Association's (ALA's) Annual Conference on June 15, 2002.

Calishain, Tara. "New Google Answers Service Raises a Few Questions of Its Own." *Information Today* 19, no. 6 (June 2002): 50–51.

Girvin Strategic Branding and Design. "Virtual Reference Services: Marketing Guidelines." January 2003. http://www.statelib.wa.gov/libraries/virtualRef/textdocs/MarketingGuidelines.pdf. Step-by-step procedures for implementing a marketing program for virtual reference services, with suggested approaches for both academic and public libraries.

Guenther, Kim. "Building Digital Libraries: Know Thy Remote Users." *Computers in Libraries* 21, no. 4 (April 2001): 52–55. Suggests strategies for working proactively to understand your remote users' needs and how they use your service in order to guide decision making about products and services for them.

Institute of Museum and Library Services. "Library Reference Goes Live on the Net, Available 24/7." http://www.imls.gov/closer/archive/hlt_10801.htm. A concise discussion of how digital reference service has evolved in libraries.

Janes, Joseph. "What Is Reference For?" Presentation at the Reference and User Services Association (RUSA) forum on the "Future of Reference Services," ALA Annual Conference, Atlanta, June 2002. http://www.ala.org/Content/NavigationMenu/RUSA/Professional_Tools4/Future_of_Reference_Services/What_Is_Reference_For_.htm.

Kasowitz, Abby. "Promoting Information Problem Solving in Digital Reference Responses." April 20, 1998. http://www.vrd.org/training/ips.shtml. Suggestions for how the Big 6 information literacy model can be promoted within a virtual reference environment.

Lipow, Anne. "Point-of-Need Reference Service: No Longer an Afterthought." Presentation at the RUSA forum on the "Future of Reference Services," ALA Annual Conference, Atlanta, June 2002. http://www.ala.org/Content/NavigationMenu/RUSA/Professional_Tools4/Future_of_Reference_Services/Point-of-Need_Reference_Service.htm.

———. "Serving the Remote User: Reference Service in the Digital Environment." http://www.csu.edu.au/special/online99/proceedings99/200.htm. Keynote address at the Information Online Conference, January 1999. As library resources and users change, the need for personalized, human-delivered reference service is greater than ever. New models of reference service will help revitalize the position of the library in its community.

Maxwell, Nancy Kalikow. "Establishing and Maintaining Live Online Reference Service." *Library Technology Reports* 38, no. 4 (July–August 2002): 1–76. A lengthy and well-researched overview of live online reference in all its facets.

McClure, Charles R., and R. David Lankes. "Assessing Quality in Digital Reference: A Research Prospectus." January 12, 2001. http://quartz.syr.edu/quality/. A research project and book on methods of assessment of virtual reference service. Provides helpful background on why measures and quality standards are important and necessary.

Reference and User Services Association, "Guidelines for Behavioral Performance of Reference and Information Services Professionals." http://www.ala.org/ala/rusa/rusaprotocols/referenceguide/guidelinesbehavioral.htm.

The Teaching Librarian: Digital Reference [website]. http://pages.prodigy.net/tabo1/digref.htm. A good site for information on virtual reference service. Includes a helpful glossary and links to other resources.

Virtual Reference Desk [website]. http://www.vrd.org/index.shtml. The Virtual Reference Desk (VRD), a project sponsored by the U.S. Department of Education, is dedicated to the advancement of virtual reference and the successful creation and operation of human-mediated, Internet-based information services. The website is an excellent source for future reference and current awareness.

Wasik, Joann M. "Digital Reference Evaluation." June 30, 2003. http://www.vrd.org/AskA/digref_assess.shtml. An Aska digest on digital reference assessment and evaluation.

Wenzel, Sarah G., and Lisa Horowitz. "Marketing Virtual Reference: Is Discretion Still the Better Part of Valor?" November 12, 2001. [PowerPoint presentation.] http://www.vrd.org/conferences/VRD2001/proceedings/wenzell.shtml. Using marketing theory as a context, this 2001 VRD Conference presentation explores issues relating to the promotion of digital reference services.

Whitlatch, Jo Bell. "Evaluating Reference Services in the Electronic Age." *Library Trends* 50, no. 2 (fall 2001): 207–19. Evaluation of virtual reference service should continue to be based on the principles used to evaluate traditional face-to-face reference services and printed reference tools. These traditional methods include surveys, questionnaires, observation, interviews, and case studies, which can be modified for use in the electronic environment.

RECOMMENDED READINGS

Bernie Sloan's Home Page [website]. http://alexia.lis.uiuc.edu/~b-sloan/home.html. A doctoral student in library and information science at the University of Illinois, Bernie Sloan has been very active in virtual reference service. The bibliographies on this site are particularly comprehensive.

"Evaluation of VRS at the University of Guelph." http://www.lib.uoguelph.ca/reference/VRD/vrdevaluation.html. This page features a number of tools used at the University of Guelph (Ontario, Can.) in the evaluation of their virtual reference service.

Francoeur, Stephen, and Lisa Ellis. "Information Competency Standards in Chat Reference Services." November 12, 2001. [PowerPoint presentation.] http://www.vrd.org/conferences/VRD2001/proceedings/francoeur.shtml. An analysis of chat reference transcripts in light of information competency standards.

Helfer, Doris Small. "Virtual Reference in Libraries: Status and Issues." *Searcher* 11, no. 2 (February 2003): 63–66.

Janes, Joseph, Chrystie Hill, and Alex Rolfe. "Ask-an-Expert Services Analysis." *Journal of the American Society for Information Science and Technology* 52, no. 13 (November 2001): 1106–21. Discusses the emergence of non-library "expert" services on the Web; compares response rates, response times, and verifiable answers for these services.

Karon, Boyd. "Why Publicize Your Library's Virtual Reference Service?" June 16, 2002. [PowerPoint presentation.] http://www.soter. net/library. Strategies for marketing libraries' virtual reference services.

Meola, Marc, and Sam Stormont. *Starting and Operating Live Virtual Reference Services.* New York: Neal-Schuman, 2002. Chapter 6, "Deciding on a Staffing Model," provides good background material for examining online staff policies.

Sterne, Jim. *Customer Service on the Internet*. New York: Wiley and Sons, 2000. Chapter 2, "Customer Service in a Modern World," and chapter 5, "Encouraging Customer Conversations," are particularly relevant to virtual reference service.

Weissman, Sara K. "E-Ref Characteristics." http://www.gti.net/weissman/character.html. Observations on virtual reference from the Morris County Library in New Jersey.

West, Jessamyn. "Information for Sale: My Experience with Google Answers." *Searcher* 10, no. 9 (October 2002): 14–17.

Whitlatch, Jo Bell. "Reference Futures: Outsourcing, the Web, or Knowledge Counseling." Presentation at the RUSA forum on the "Future of Reference Services," ALA Annual Conference, Atlanta, June 2002. http://www.ala.org/rusa/forums/whitlatch_forum.html. Discusses choices in the design and management of reference service and how they might determine the future of reference service.

INDEX

BUFF HIRKO is Statewide Virtual Reference Project coordinator, Washington State Library, Olympia. She coordinates grant demonstration projects, training, marketing, evaluation, and other activities focused on the development of digital reference service in Washington libraries. Since receiving her M.L.S. from the University of California at Berkeley, she has worked in public, academic, and special libraries in California, Germany, North Carolina, and Washington State. She is a frequent speaker at state and national conferences and is a regular contributor to library publications.

MARY BUCHER ROSS manages staff training and development at the Seattle Public Library. She designs and presents library staff training and continuing education programs for the Washington State Library, the Washington Library Association, and the University of Washington. Her master's degree in library and information science is from the University of California at Los Angeles. In addition to the Anytime, Anywhere Answers program, she has designed workshops introducing the concepts of virtual reference to library directors and reference staff who are not currently providing the service.